SONNET

FOR BROOKS PITT

WHO KEEPS ME PRETTY!

A MEMOIR OF FAMILY DYSFUNCTION

G.H. LARRIVEE JR.

Outskirts Press, Inc.
Denver, Colorado

SonSet
A Memoir of Family Dysfunction

v3.0

Outskirts Press, Inc.
http://www.outskirtspress.com

ISBN: 978-1-4327-4641-4

PRINTED IN THE UNITED STATES OF AMERICA

CONTENTS

For Carolyn,
from whom all my blessings flow

For Samantha and Jack

For Me:
...if I get it all down on paper
it's no longer inside of me
threatnin' the life it belongs to...
Anna Nylick
Breathe/2 AM

Glossary of Terms

*Gig – four wheels on a board

*Scott – self - contained air

*Booster line – ¾ or 1″ rubber hose on a hose-reel on a fire truck

*IMH – Institute of Mental Health

*Code; Code 99 – a state of cardiac arrest; so named because 99% died

*Trendelenberg – shock position; head down, feet up

*CNA – Certified Nursing Assistant; tends to the physical well-being of a patient

The Principals

Some years ago the mother of the grandchildren I have never met took it upon herself to engage in a brief e-mail exchange. I was taken entirely by surprise, but I'm not hard to find and I suppose I had always known there would someday be an inquiry because their children are asking difficult questions. My son's wife needs to satisfy herself that all is just as she has come to understand - that I am indeed the distant and recalcitrant ogre that no one really needs to know.

By the time we had packed up our memories and headed west, my son was having nothing much to do with us. Before I drew up my retirement papers I approached him one more time with an offer to help him complete his business degree at any one of a number of quality schools. His response at the time was:

"What makes you think I'd ask you for anything".

The other half of "we" is Carolyn, my wife of thirty years. We met in the ER of Rhode Island Hospital just before I was promoted to be a fire department rescue company officer and we've been together ever since. Think romance novel, television pilot, chick flick – all at once and double it. We revel in the good fortune of finding each other. We laugh together, we cry together and we hold each other up. We can also rag on each other relentlessly and expose the barest nerve. We are not good at being apart and we marvel that military couples make it at all. Come at either one of us, you'd have to take us both because we can indeed circle one wagon.

Another part of Carolyn is Bob. He was ten when we met and he was so excited to finally get to have a father that his real one showed up - and none too soon, either. The guy had finally figured out that despite his disregard over the years, the kid still wanted him and still needed his father to want him in return. Bob's father managed that illusion just well enough to dispel any influence that me and Carolyn might have had. The resulting vacuum allowed Bob the opportunity to choose his own way with almost no forethought whatsoever.

KJ's mother and I had found ourselves with child, married at eighteen, and we were done only a few years later. I was angry and frustrated and the split was ugly and bitter and no one was spared the fallout. Some people took sides and almost no one took hers - I made sure of it. KJ would rally to her side and he would create a formidable opposition in her defense, and so it came to be that the child who would always be mine wouldn't piss on me now if I was on fire.

A Letter in Reply

My Dear Lady,

I was very much taken by the fact that your curiosity couldn't hold out any longer and that you extended yourself to find me. Your inquiry of just what kind of a father could be more involved in social causes instead of with his own son has taken me over a year to consider and much longer to write reflectively about. It has also opened wounds that took years to nearly heal. If you wrote to me expecting to find a broken and grieving man desperate for the love and attention of my son and his family, you should know first hand that our Larrivees are not made that way.

I am very frustrated that our letters were somehow put before my son. That should not have happened until you and I had nothing left to explore. My forthright opinions would truly lead you to conclude that I am indeed *the* kind of person my progeny would describe to you. Had you read between the lines a little, you would have realized that there is so much more at work here than anything you've been told. This is not a situation where you can presume or believe without reservation. This is an estrangement that began long before the time in Reno when my son allowed us the privilege of his surly presence.

I suppose that my greatest regret is that KJ never really cared enough to look at any side but his own. It is my bad that I allowed the bitterest of emotions to get to me on a continuing basis and there was certainly enough overflow to poison the waters around us. By the time I realized what shouldn't have gone on, my son was long gone by any measure of a connection, never to return. All he ever wanted from me throughout his childhood was to leave him to his mother or else just leave him alone. He clings mostly to what he decided when he was a toddler and I probably gave him little opportunity to feel otherwise.

What I most resent is how manipulated we had always been made to feel. Carolyn and I tried to create a family unit that would provide the warmth and the values that we both wanted for our children, while at the same time fulfilling the career ambitions that we all would benefit from. Seemed like a pretty good plan; couldn't have gone more awry. Instead of cooperation we had one child trying to elbow his way in and the other trying to slam the door on him. As they eventually learned to keep each other's secrets, they collectively became a whole new force to reckon with. Add the spoiling effects of the other parent, and dissent became the new way of life.

I was taken by your observation that we Larrivees just open fire and those first thoughts come barreling out. My Larrivees have been doing this for generations now and getting away with it, especially when we follow it up with whatever will back you off. My son is no longer a child; he's damn near 40. He is in charge of his own fusillade - once forgiven for his youth - but no longer for the bitter and indeterminate broadsides. He chooses to remain ignorant or dishonest and entirely out of touch with his own responsibility for what became of us. Most of what you think you know has little to do with my take on the history that my son would describe as emotional abandonment. What I did in fact, was to stop going the extra mile for someone who was always headed the other way. My son did exactly what he wanted to do by unfairly castigating Carolyn as he did. I had found a way to co-exist with that and with all of the grievances that had kept me tied to his whipping post. Since you have chosen to inquire, I now choose to share.

The Early Years

It seems that I have been awarded a number of lives, but I ran right through a few just trying to survive childhood. I am the second grandson of Gian B. Caito Jr. who was 52 in '52 and I am the first born of his only daughter, Carolyn Jane. I have one sister and three brothers. Two of the brothers are twins, and not only do they not look anything alike, they don't even qualify as brothers. One is a two – fisted tattooed biker wacko with a history of every imaginable abuse he could inflict upon himself and everybody around him. There's a story that he once jumped on the hood of a guy's car with a chain saw and may or may not have made just a little hole. Now he's ordained himself a minister. The other half is a cerebral genius who holds at least one advanced degree, speaks a couple of languages and teaches at an institution of higher learning somewhere in Maine. They were raised together as Dad's little slaves, working the land because they had no choice, the rest of us being mostly grown and gone. They were always referred to or described as "the twins" and shortly after they were born Mom descended into a living hell of surgically induced misery and depression. Dad was never there for her and even when he was, he could only manage to be insulting and degrading. No one was spared; Dad was an equal opportunity despot and when he was around, we made ourselves scarce. He had a particular dislike reserved only for me, and there were times when I feared for my life at his hand.

I never knew my other grandfather because he died when Dad was six. Dad said he was sick for a long time but others say he drank a lot. To me, it is all one and the same if in fact both suppositions are correct. He was about 50 when he died – born in 1886. All of the remaining photos show him in WW I campaign garb although he may not have completed his enlistment. He was much older than his wife – my grandmother – who died of colon cancer in 1954. Together they had four children, one of whom died in adolescence. They moved quite often; whether it was to beat the rent or the law is unknown. Nobody's sayin'.

Dad was a big strong truck driver who fancied himself a horseman and a farmer and he would describe himself as the toughest guy who ever lived. He maintained a reputation for or perhaps an illusion of clobbering people left and right and no one I knew would ever say otherwise. When Muhammed Ali was champion of the world, Dad used to go on about wanting "a coupla rounds to teach that nigger a thing or two" quite publicly. And we kids were all in awe, *because he was our dad;* the biggest and strongest and toughest of men among men. And all of his buddies that I ever knew were real men, too. I wondered what they were like at home.

I was almost nine when the twins were born and shortly thereafter, Mom went in for a hysterectomy that nearly killed her. She was 31 years old, had never suffered ill health, and suddenly she wasn't there and Gram was. Post - op, she developed a number of complications and she was hospitalized for quite a long time. Dad divided his time between going to work and going to the hospital and we rarely saw him. When Mom finally came home she took to her bed and emerged a shell of the woman we had always known. She lived on coffee, cigarettes and green medicine and forever after she didn't care if she lived or died. As soon as she seemed well enough, Dad went back to not being around much.

Hormonal therapy had yet to be discovered and Mom essentially entered early menopause from the hysterectomy. She was an old woman by the time she was 40 and she died at 53. The etiology is well documented today. Most women are somewhat protected from early heart disease by the hormones that they naturally produce. At menopause, women enter the same realm of risk for heart disease as that of men. Two packs of cigarettes a day over a lifetime of careless living created a recipe for personal disaster. Mom developed calcified arteries in her heart that defied the apparatus they used to pound through it. Instead, the catheter broke off and they had to retrieve it during by-pass surgery. I think she never wanted to wake up, and she never did.

Back in the days when men were men and women were glad of it, I grew up largely clueless about anything of real importance. We used to live on Cartier St. where it was very dark most of the time. Maybe I got put down for a nap more than I should have. That would make it seem dark most of the time. It's like how deep the snow used to be – you forget how short you were. There is an early black and white photo of me sitting on a slab of cement at the new house on Charcalee drive. I was very little. What the photo doesn't show is the manner in which I was scooped up like a loose football and planted on the new front steps.

"NOW STAY THERE !!!"

The bulldozer that would have mashed me into pulp is also not shown.

Life on Charcalee Dr. got me a dog and a pony and grandparents bearing candy just down the street. There were deep woods behind us where plenty of bears could hide and that kept us kind of close until we knew better. Then me and my cousins next door would leave Shorty with Mom and disappear before she could realize she was stuck with him. We didn't care; he was always too little. And my sister certainly wasn't welcome nor any other girls if there ever were any.

At Mrs. Pike's nursery school we got grape Kool-Aid, played outside on monkey bars, and we all had to pee in a wastebasket. A really old lady would make the boys line up one after another to pee in this thing. It had a foot pedal that popped the top open and sometimes we'd cross swords two or three at a time. It was great.

I went to kindergarten at Meshanticut Park School where some girl named Phyllis hated me and Danny O'Brien pushed me down and then said he didn't and I had to get stitches. Miss King had us all take a turn at a butter churn, and then after she spread the butter on Ritz crackers, no one would eat it. We all knew that butter came in sticks and whatever the hell we just made sure wasn't butter. I was always a fussy eater; Mom needed to hear old Dr. Donahue say that peanut butter was O.K. and that Cheerios were even better. We'd go to his office where he'd fill the doorway to the waiting room and look around for who was next:

"How ya' doin', handsome!" he'd bellow.

Then we'd walk with him and Mom towards the smell of needles.

Once I got to St. Ann's School, life got serious. We had nuns who we called "Sister" like they all shared the same first name. Actually, they had mostly taken some of the prettiest sounding names that except for those of all of the saints, didn't make any sense. Sister Daniel Patrick took the names of two men who must surely be saints but why are the nuns taking *men's names*? And Sister Rose Terrence; where'd that come from? Sister Julia was a gentle giant and Sister Annunciata loved to talk about horses with me. But first grade got me Sister Helena.

Sr. Helena St. James was a bantam weight terrorist who would condemn some of us to hell in a heartbeat if it were up to her. I would be first followed closely by Michael Alba, Richard Salzillo, and Donna Paolino's mom. I was always guilty of something even when I wasn't because I was left handed and Sister Helena could always see the devil's tail wrapped around my legs. Richard Salzillo laughed at her until she tried to beat him to death with a hickory pointer, and then he laughed even more. He was the biggest kid in the class. Michael Alba just looked out the window most of the time. He was even more bored with school than I was and he didn't bother to hide it. In class, I was busy riding horses and herding cattle while next door cousin sat far away across the room learning what we were supposed to. And Donna Paolino's mother simply came to pick up her daughter for an appointment or something and Sister Helena wouldn't let her go. It got pretty heated with Sister Helena saying "Oh, No. She's God's child and you can't have her". This went on until Mrs. Paolino got the Mother Superior to persuade Sister Helena that she had to let go.

We prayed over everything. A buzzer on the wall used to go off and we'd pray. Any time the fire trucks down the street went out, we'd have to pray for whatever poor soul they were going to rescue. We prayed before lunch and again right after and we prayed when we dove under our desks during "duck and cover" drills. When they marched us up to St Ann's Church during Lent or holy days, we prayed about going and we prayed for a safe return. We even prayed as we marched past the old stinkriver that the print works used to liberally pollute. Once, I tried to slide through the iron bars where the road went over the river and got smacked in the behind for my audacity.

We were hooked on phonics before it ever became the rage and I once spelled "uv" on a test just because I was the devils child, me being left handed and all. But I couldn't tell you the first thing about why Catholic is catholic all by itself as a religion except that they have the Vatican. And Jews were a tribe or a breed; very foreign and very bad except for when Jesus was a Jew. Sister Helena got all red in the face when I asked her what a Protestant was and she told us that it was *almost* a sin to be with one. And Dad, who wasn't Catholic (except for when he had to be to marry Mom), used to listen to what I came home with and sent me back to school with a few ideas of his own. Since he was DAD, it never bothered me to parrot stuff back at the nuns and once it got me sentenced to the parallelogram.

The parallelogram was actually the boiler room that was right across the hall from the incinerator and around the corner from Mother Superior's office. It was dark and hot and really scary and if you were bad enough you got yourself locked in there for a while. The reputation of the place struck fear into the hearts of anyone who would still believe in Santa Claus and the bigger kids made it sound even worse. I got taken to the parallelogram once and when Sister opened the door, I bolted down the hall. Since I didn't dare leave the school or the grounds, I became my own hostage. I truly thought I would die that day, if they ever told Dad.

Meanwhile back at the ranch, Mom had just won me a pony in the Sealtest Ice Cream "Name the Seal" contest. I think she won with "Sparky" because that's what it said on the package. I was in the second grade and I was so proud because I got to feed and water Lucky and a number of other horses twice a day through the winter. Dad had just scored a union job which was a big deal then and being low man, Dad got the crummy hours so he was never there to help with the horses. Some times I would curl up on the rug at the back door with my dog Laddie and sleep there until he got home so he could carry me to bed. I don't blame Dad for making that stop, though. He couldn't get the door open with us laying there.

We got into the horse show business for just long enough to win some third, fourth, and fifth place ribbons. I got one second place and tied for a first place ribbon once with a girl named Gerry Boylan who usually won everything. We were eight or nine years old. Towards the end it got pretty ugly since I wasn't doing so hot in school, being the devil's left handed child and all. The practice sessions during the week were a horror. Dad was incredibly profane and mistakes at 5:30 in the morning before school were always enough to get him to unload. Add that to my schoolwork and I became "nothin' but a goddam nitwit." Never mind that he didn't really know how we were supposed to show a horse. Turns out, there was actual prize money but I never saw any. We quit showing Lucky after Dad decided that we'd probably never win much and he needed to be away even more. I didn't care. I was mostly in it for the grape sodas you could get for a nickel and a chance to see Paladin from "Have Gun Will Travel". Besides, there wouldn't be any more of those pre-school sessions and I could stop being scared for a while, so long as I didn't get caught using all those bad words.

At St. Ann's School Dennis McConaghy tagged me with "Laahhh TV" by the second grade. "That kid always acts like he's on TV" he used to say. The nuns all called me "Professor" since I always had an answer or an explanation or an excuse. Dennis and I were the two trouble makers on the school bus and Mike the bus driver made us sit right behind him all the time. He said our next step was to have to sit with the girls but when I eschewed a lunger out the window and got Ray Stoehr's brother in the head, I was off the bus. Dennis thought it was hilarious; Dad would not. Somehow Mom and Gram managed to keep this away from Dad while Gram took me to school and after a while I was back on the bus. When Dennis started talking about the giant hat pin he was going to get Mike back with, I got a little light-headed.

In second grade I had to get eyeglasses. The doctor said I had a lazy eye and I had to wear a patch to make it stronger. They wouldn't let me have a pirate's patch; I had to have one that clipped on over my glasses and everybody called me "four eyes". Later on, a lot of kids had to get glasses while I was getting rid of mine. And I never got braces.

In third grade we got Mrs. Needham for a teacher instead of a nun. This was just starting to take hold in Catholic schools since the supply of nuns was drying up. Imagine the application process to be a Catholic lay teacher in those days of Vatican II turmoil. They had just given up on the meatless Fridays rule and even abandoned a few saints. Some of the lesser mortal sins were dismissed, the Mass would now be in English and the priest would face the crowd. And so it followed that we wouldn't even be taught in Catholic school by a bona fide nun. They were just starting to lose Catholics, but they lost me for good when Sister Helena said I couldn't have Laddie in heaven. Laddie was a *good* dog. He even bit Dad for hitting me.

I lost my best friend Robbie Thompson. We were best pals forever and we did everything two kids aren't supposed to. We went near the pond next to his house before we could swim and we got lost in the woods once just before nightfall. And it was his woods so I wasn't paying attention to how far we went and we both got in trouble. We played baseball in the summer and went sledding in the winter and we explored a prehistoric swamp that I was sure would swallow us up if a T-Rex didn't. We watched Louie Heinhold turn an outhouse into splinters with the coolest looking grenade that a kid could ever manufacture and then we never saw Louie Heinhold again. Robbie had two older sisters that we didn't even spy on because Robbie said they'd kill us and besides, we didn't have to prove anything to *any old girls*. All I could tell you is that one wasn't blonde and they weren't fat and we didn't care any more about them than we did about anybody else's sisters. I always thought I'd get old knowing Robbie Thompson because life is supposed to go just like on TV where nothing really bad happens. Instead, Mrs. Jansen killed herself, Johnny Ekdahl's father died, and Mom got sick. Then Robbie Thompson moved away.

I retreated into TV land like everybody else with burgeoning ADD. By the time I got to fourth grade I was mired in a western fantasy cowboy life that I only needed to run off and join since I already had my horse. I was already a really good reader and Mom got me into a series called "The Real Book About…" A new book would come every month but I'd read them all over and over, sometimes under the covers with a flashlight. Then I'd daydream in school until Miss Valentine decided otherwise and she really got my attention. After Dad yanked us from Catholic school we went to Meshanticut Park Elementary School where I had gone to kindergarten and where Dad went as a kid and Miss Valentine was also *his* fourth grade teacher. At first I was terrified because Dad knew Miss Valentine and that she'd rat me out about every miscreant deed. It never happened. Miss Valentine was tall and strong and hard and would handle me just fine by herself. One time I said something stupid or insulting or both and Miss Valentine clocked me so hard that I fell right out of my chair.

At parent teacher conferences that Mom and Gram went to, Miss Valentine would go on about my being so smart. I had struggled at St. Ann's what with being so busy as a cowboy and all and I got into a lot of trouble, mostly for fighting. Dad and Mother Superior had agreed that I wouldn't be sorely missed and that Dad would be wasting his money when the diocese started charging tuition the next year. They had him at the "charge tuition" part since it apparently it had always been free to parish members. But if public school was good enough for Dad, it was suddenly good enough for his kids. And it would have been too if we didn't have to attend catechism class two or three afternoons a week *with Sister Helena*. Once, they tried to move catechism class to Saturdays but they got off of that pretty quick. Nothing could compete with Saturday morning television.

About half way through the fourth grade of public school I was declared a genius. I never wanted this or meant for it to happen or even took any stock in it but everybody else did and Mom was so proud. I certainly didn't feel any smarter than anyone else (well maybe a little) and in fact, I wasn't. It was just that Catholic school was always so far ahead of public school because the nuns could really hurt you if you defied learning. In fourth grade I was garnering A's without breaking a sweat because I had had it all before. This went on until about half way into the fifth grade where it all caught up with me. Even though Miss Frederick would never even *think* to hit anybody, I had lost my ability to easily excel. Then I became the "laziest, nit wit son of a bitch" Dad could have for a son. When A's became B's on their way to C's and D's, Mom and I both got caught in the backfire. She was once a math wiz who worked in a bank but they changed how they taught math and it became the "new" math that nobody's parents could help with. Mom really tried – spent hours with me so Dad would stop yelling.

We figured out some of it together but there would never again be the straight A's and Dad would never be proud of me. I had figured out that Dad really hated me – probably would kill me off if he could – but Mom might miss me and Gram would call the cops. It was the worst time of my life so far and at night when I said my prayers I'd beg God to just whisk me away to wherever He was. If a space ship ever landed, I'd have got on it. Then they'd be sorry.

After I got out of Mrs. Barney's Cub Scout den, I got into WEBLOS which is big- boy Cub Scouts but just before *real* Boy Scouts. "We B Loyal Scouts" is what they said WEBLOS meant. Our leader was another Mr. Thompson who was probably one of the smartest guys who ever had to work an everyday job when he really should have been president. His kid was the genius I was supposed to be and sometimes we didn't get along so well, mostly because I cleaned him out in poker games at camp. In WEBLOS, I imagine we were supposed to be doing something worthwhile but mostly we played this massive game of "team keep-away" in the Thompson's cluttered basement while we listened to Providence College games on radio. Almost everything I know about basketball came from Mr. Thompson because he was an enormous fan of Providence College. They were a national powerhouse in the days when they really had to run, dribble and shoot being short and white and all. There was this one guy – Vinny Ernst; they said he'd be the next Bob Cousy but by the time he graduated PC, you had to be able to dunk the ball.

One evening just before I got on the real fire department, Mr. Thompson set himself on fire as he drove up the road with a dead woman next to him. Dead at the scene, both burned to a crisp. One of the cops who was chasing him saw the whole thing. Unbelievable; as smart as that guy was, you'd think he would have done something a whole lot less gruesome. But just as probable would be that he simply had himself an overwhelming breakdown over everything that adds up to unbearable. Either way, it was pretty dramatic and I felt pretty badly about it and I can think of about half a dozen other people I'd gladly cheer on doing it. Too bad it wasn't Dad.

I moved on to Boy Scouts and joined Troop Six, Cranston. Best thing I ever did and if I wasn't the best Boy Scout who ever lived, I was certainly in the top two. Mom didn't drive so I used to bum a ride with Gramp who went to Kiwanis Club dinner meetings a bit earlier on Thursday nights. Boy Scouts was at the fire station at seven o'clock and he'd drop me off at six so I'd kill an hour across the street listening to Mike DeSoscio practice his accordion. I was always welcome in that house. Mr. DeSoscio always used to say:

"It's always a pleasure to shake hands with a gentleman".

I don't know if he really meant that I was a gentleman, or if he simply wanted me to be one. But he always shook my hand.

In fifth grade I had Miss Frederick and I had never met a nicer lady who just happened to be a teacher. Being so young and all, Miss Frederick's unmarriedness meant nothing until I was a rescue lieutenant responding to a master box alarm at the school where she was now principal. She was standing on the sidewalk being the principal when I moseyed up to her and said:

"Hello, Miss Frederick..."

Miss Frederick hadn't changed a whole lot in 20 years and now she whirled around, eyes wide, about a hundred kids staring at us both. I re-introduced myself so she wouldn't feel pressed to remember and for a moment she couldn't find words. Then she presented me to all of these kids as this really good student she'd had before she was MRS. SIMONE. It seemed like she couldn't really go back to when she *was* Miss Frederick, but I sure could. Seeing her surrounded by those kids, I loved her once again. She was the first adult I was never afraid of.

I got somewhat back on track with my schoolwork in the fifth grade and Boy Scouts opened up a whole new world that helped me keep clear of Dad. By now he was on the road almost all the time but he wasn't a long haul driver like the guys who live in their trucks. He had a run he'd do from Lincoln, R.I. to parts of New York, New Jersey, and Pennsylvania. The company put him up in the Times Square Hotel so he could steal towels and they gave him a meal allowance that he kept for all those other times when he wasn't home. Mom hated the whole situation what with five kids and all but the money was really good and really necessary. When Dad was home, he slept almost all of the time except for when he was yelling at the new man of the house.

Mom didn't get her drivers license until just before I did and it was always a serious handicap. Gram had to drive her and us anytime Dad couldn't (which was always) and living out in the country kept us home a lot. I couldn't play little league baseball or pee wee football and hockey practice was every day at five or six in the morning all the way across town. I played a lot of sand lot and even Kevin Barney would say that I had a stinger of a fast ball and he used to stop hockey pucks. Still, if you don't start these sports early, you have to make a hell of an impression to get noticed later on. The high school coaches already pretty much know who their stars are going to be. I ran at half - back way behind Mark VanEeghen and he went on to play for the Oakland Raiders. Dad had this idea that I was going to be the football hero that he had been. It didn't matter that I was the runt of his litter; Uncle Maury was a standout at Brown University at 155 pounds – one of the original "Iron Men". I was the oldest and I'd just have to find a way to get it done. He'd get really mouthy about my playing football. He badgered Mom into getting her driver's license so she could pick me up from practice that first year. He bragged that when I made the team my first year of high school football, he'd buy me a car.

Whoa!

That got my attention. Nobody I knew was getting a car handed to them. It put my next door uncle in a bit of a spot for my next door cousin, but Dad didn't care. He'd go on and on until that Christmas we were at Gramps house and Uncle Steve the Austrian said to him:

"GERARD! Look at the size of him!
Don't you care about your children?!"

Gram also jumped in since she was already dead set against my football career and she never let up about it to Mom, either. So Dad shut up and I played football although "play" isn't really the watch word here. Mostly, me and Bill Boyle stood together on the sidelines wishing we were Van Eeghen. My nick-name was "O.J." and I got my car, but only because Coach Orabone never cut anybody.

Sixth Grade

Meshanticut Park Elementary School was a mix of religious persuasion in Cranston, R.I in those days. That whole line of thinking about how Catholics always want to know if you're Catholic was true enough for me because I always found myself asking. Everyone in Meshanticut wasn't Catholic and everyone didn't go to church *every* Sunday. We knew a couple of Jewish kids but we had no idea of what that was about until Sister told us that they didn't believe in Jesus. Protestant kids didn't *have* to go to church every Sunday - wasn't even a sin! I felt kind of screwed because for us not only was there weekly Mass, there were catechism classes all week as well. Protestant kids went to Sunday school during the church service itself, wrapping up their weekly obligation in about an hour and a half. We were just learning about this brave new way when the world I had grown accustomed to fell completely apart. It seems that my parents weren't the only ones to reject the new Catholic school tuition plan, and now the city found itself awash in more new students to provide for. Since they couldn't just fabricate a school or two right away, the only alternative was to re-distribute the load. This came as our reassignment to the Thornton Elementary School in the northwest corner of Cranston, an area we had never even *heard* of. It was populated with first and second generation Italian households; homes where Italian was spoken language. These kids had been going to this school all along and most of us transplants had to make our own way socially. Once, a really tall kid named Angelo bumped his morning wood against me in line but aside from my being perfectly mortified, nothing else happened. Angelo thought it was funny.

Also that year would be The BEATLES and every girl had a Beatles lunch box or a three ring binder and maybe even a fantasy.

I got to see the *real* inside of my leg for the first time which made my first stitches in kindergarten seem like a scratch. I blame it all on the teacher's strike because if school had opened when it was supposed to, none of this would have happened. I would have been safely tucked in my seat instead of fooling around with a rip saw and opening up my leg with it. Dad was really pissed but when he saw the size of the hole, even he got a little scared. It was filling up with blood, but it really was something to see your actual insides. Dad took me to the hospital where I had to take my pants off in front of a *woman* doctor and I got eleven stitches.

At Thornton Elementary, everybody was very Catholic and more Italian than I had ever known and I'm part Italian from Gramp's whole side. GreatGramma was Gramp's mom and she didn't speak English although Gram said she understood it just fine. If you asked Dad he'd brag about the French in us but if you asked Father Allaire, he'd probably say I was part of the Canuck riff-raff that murdered the French language. He used to call me "Mr. Larriviere" and turned away with his nose in the air when I corrected him. Father Allaire carried himself as a true intellectual. Had real money, too.

One thing I observed at that time was that it was pretty easy to get into a fight at Thornton Elementary School. These were pretty big kids who fought a lot and I was pretty scrawny and they mostly left me alone. Nobody really needed to see what a scrapper I was because I was a tough guy by reputation and they must've known it. Either that or they never gave me a second thought. Only Kevin Barney dared to take me on in a neighborhood rivalry that ended with a head injury. Kevin and I never threw big punches at each other because we always used to be friends but this was serious work. He had walked all the way up from his bus stop a half a mile away just to show me that he would. We were very seriously not thumping each other when I went down hard and headlong into the remains of a really big tree stump they had left in the fork of Council Rock Road. I was loopy all the way to school; should have been hospitalized.

Another Gerry was the bravest, toughest, most alienated kid to ever walk the halls of that school and he was my friend. He had muscles I wished I had and there wasn't anybody he couldn't take down hard if he wanted to. He was a little older for some reason, maybe about 14. Thornton Elementary only went to sixth grade yet Gerry was already a young man. He had a little problem with aggression, and anger management hadn't yet been invented. Like a pit bull, Gerry learned violence and then it became his habitat. He lived a couple of miles up the road from me and we were country kids who did the same kind of farm work growing up and that's about all we had in common along with abusive fathers. Gerry taught me and Johnny Palermo how to break pencils across our knuckles until there were no more pencils.

One time in the dining hall Gerry had a spat with a cocky teacher who thought he'd drag a little respect out of this punk kid. Whatever the issue was, it didn't actually matter since this thing was going to happen right in front of us and Mr. Teacher probably had no idea of what he was up against. They were right in each other's faces when Gerry suddenly turned and stalked out of the dining room. Through the double doors, one was closed and with a palm heel strike he busted it right off two of its' three hinges. Unfathomable at the time; it was an extraordinary event. Beyond awesome. Me and Johnny Palermo couldn't have been more amazed – or proud. When Gerry's father came to the school to address the issue he walked straight up to where they had his son sitting in a chair and clocked him hard across the face, screaming at him all the while. I was in the hallway watching this from the beginning to almost the end and thinking how it could have been me. The beating part, that is. It got worse for Gerry because once again Mr. Teacher pushed him too far only this time he got his head split for his trouble. I didn't see it and there were conflicting accounts about how it started but everybody agrees that Mr. Teacher got dropped like a rock and took some stitches. I remember being pretty smug about how my pal had tuned up a teacher who really needed it but we never saw Gerry again.

I got introduced to real music that year. Mr. Olivieri taught brass and woodwinds and there was never a doubt that I would be an accomplished trumpet player. I followed Al Hirt and Satchmo and Herb Alpert and I bought a pile of their sheet music. There were about a half dozen of us who got out of regular class to take music lessons and I would practice every day. Mom loved "Silver Bells" at Christmas and I always brought the horn to play at Gramp's Christmas gala and my sister Jazzy would play piano. Uncle Steve the Austrian thought we were great, and he was a serious student of classical violin.

Mr. Hickey taught accelerated science and English but only to those who could qualify for his individual attention. He required an essay that would capture his interest with the very first sentence and then he would go about changing the content of everything the author meant. He was a very difficult teacher to please, especially if you didn't agree with his assessments so I didn't last in that class long enough to learn anything except to stand up for my own thoughts.

Kennedy died that year. They say that everybody knows exactly where they were and exactly what they were doing when Kennedy died. When Mr. Pepin came out and told Mr. Flynn, we were on the asphalt schoolyard in front of Thornton Elementary playing a new form of baseball that about a hundred kids could play at once and still qualify as phys-ed. You'd hit this big rubber ball out of your hand and try to get to first base but there were always so many kids in the field and the ball was so large that only the biggest kids could hit it past them. The fielders could throw the ball at you to get you out and they even let the girls play. It was pretty lame and we mostly didn't care when they made us all go back in to listen about Kennedy. But everybody had to have phys- ed because of television; they actually made it a law.

We stayed home from school and watched the funeral, hours

and hours that my being a Boy Scout felt required to observe. Everything was closed except police, fire and NORAD and the country entered a period of national mourning. It was a little more difficult for Mom's side of the family because her uncle was U.S. Senator John O. Pastore who was the keynote speaker at the Democratic National Convention that had nominated Kennedy. We mourned a little harder than everybody else except for Dad who never forgave Kennedy for his showdown with the Teamsters because it made Jimmy Hoffa blink.

Great Society

Dad didn't drink. It was LBJ and his "Great Society" that brought out the worst in Dad and he'd aim it at all of us until I learned to stay away. He was fresh off of boiling over about the showdown between JFK and the Teamsters, and he hadn't gotten to wallop anybody lately. So now he was into yelling all the time and always at me. He could really go off and it took almost no provocation; I learned to breathe real softly.

Dad hated everybody who wasn't him and no one was safe. He called Mom the "skinny guinea", told wop jokes and nigger jokes and admired the hell out of Jews because Israel never took any crap and Jews had money. Even his friends weren't immune and he'd go off about somebody's wife wearing the pants or about whose wife had too much mouth. He used to call both my Uncle Bobs' cheapskates because they had savings accounts; Dad's money was always in his pocket. What he hated worst of all was the fact that he had to go to work every day while "...niggers on welfare get to stay home and sleep when they ain't making more niggers on welfare." You could count on hearing that at least a few times a day, even though there were probably just as many white people gaming the system. But it was always open season on yours truly and anything I said or did would make Dad immediately change direction.

Just his inflection was enough to make you wilt. It would begin with "you little son of a bitch..." and you couldn't always tell if you should weather it or run. When you're eight or nine or ten, it always feels dangerous and isolated – alone in your fear. Sometimes Mom would intercede if she thought she could get to him before he got to be life - threatening, but I didn't usually wait that long. One time he chased me into the house which was stupid on my part but I was little and he could still catch me in the open field and I didn't know where else to go. I dove under one side of the kitchen table and when he grabbed for me I scrambled to the other side. Back and forth it went with Mom screaming at him not to kill me or hit me in the head. He finally hauled me out from under with such a force that I sailed across the kitchen out of his grasp and slid on my belly until I could get those little feet through the front door.

Another time we were supposed to be raking leaves from the back yard to the street in front. Autumn always sucked in our house because we had a number of huge oak trees that used to blanket the yard with leaves a foot deep. Dad would order us to rake them to the street so he could burn them except that he'd be asleep on the couch, no one dared disturb him and all the leaves would blow back. Next weekend we'd have to do it all over again. And so it went until one day when Shorty wouldn't help and I had had enough of it. I was yelling at him to help and he wouldn't and Dad must have heard the ruckus. He came out just in time to see me swing a big old branch full of leaves at Shorty and he broke into a dead run right at me. Now for a big guy, he could really move. He used to brag about being a "traveling tackle" in high school because he was so fast. That's just an old football term for pulling a guard or tackle on an end sweep, but if you're the lead blocker, you'd better be able to get out front. I took off through the woods as fast as I could run for at least a couple of hundred yards. I don't know what made me look over my shoulder as I started to ease up but he was right there and about to grab me by the shirt collar. I dug in for another quarter mile with everything I had until Dad got winded and gave up.

I lived in total fear of the man, even planned for either his death or my own. Many a time, I held his favorite carving knife in my hand thinking how easy it would be to just plunge it into his chest as he lay asleep in the other room. Maybe that was just a dream. I know I sometimes woke up thinking about it. Another time when there was no one around I found the shotgun shells that he kept hidden and taught myself to load the old Stevens just in case I wanted to. About the only thing that stopped me was that they'd put me in the bad boy's school where conditions were just horrid and I had already had a close call with that. One time we went to a horse show on the grounds of "Sockanossett" – the boys reformatory – and I innocently climbed up into the stands and sat next to some of the school's clientele. When it was time to go, they grabbed me up too and I couldn't see Dad. Scarred me for life, but that was a good thing - kept me from offing Dad or from dying in the attempt.

On Sundays, it was fun for them to pile the family into the car and go for a ride with both of them smoking and the windows rolled up because Mom was always cold. We never knew where we were headed except that we wouldn't be going out of our way for ice cream. One time, we were parked at Meshanticut Lake where everybody took their kids fishing and ice skating. Mom and Dad grew up in the area so it was a favorite for them and most of their friends. We weren't at all surprised when Billy White, the motorcycle cop, pulled along side to say "Hi". He was tall and rugged and black and he was about the most pleasant person to be around that I had ever met. He had grown up in the neighborhood, went to school with Mom and Dad, and *everybody* liked Billy White – even Gram. He went on to become a juvenile police detective and I used to see him all the time in my job. Today he took one in the gut:

MOMMY! DADDY'S TALKIN' TO A NIGGER!

Thank God it was Shorty and not me. He was only about three or four but he knew what a nigger was and he sure knew how to say so. And Mr. White seemed not to even notice, even though he had to notice plenty. "Well Gerard and Carolyn, you have a nice day now" was all he said and then he was gone. We just sat there awhile, Dad a bit red-faced and Mom a brand new shade of white. She looked over at him while he stared straight ahead.

"Happy now?"

And Shorty, once again: "But Dad, you were talkin' to a nigger!?"

"Yeah, but he's a good nigger"

Then we went home, again without ice cream.

Dad never changed. He talked of the day when George Wallace would finally get it together to be president so we could play "...cowboys and colored people". He seemed satisfied enough with the assassination of Martin Luther King, so much so that he didn't even crow about it too much. Everybody seemed to fear that it was just a matter of time for Dr. King. Even Dr. King must have known that somebody even worse than Dad would put him in the crosshairs.

Gram and Gramp always had a Christmas Eve open house downstairs in the speakeasy that Gramp built especially for big gatherings. There'd be a lot of family and extended family around and Dad toned it down a bit but he always made it clear from one year to the next that his position on niggers hadn't changed a whit. And then Uncle Steve the Austrian let him have it:

"Gerard!! What the hell'd a colored person ever do to you!!?"

The whole room froze, and then Uncle Steve said it again. And he waited for an answer. And Dad said:

"All I'm sayin' is that they might be equal to me – they ain't no better than me."

Uncle Steve was still red in the face and looked like all of his compact self was ready to come at Dad just for being so ignorant. Then Gramp called it off.

Christmastime was a festival of good cheer where Mom took comfort in her family, away from all the trying days of the rest of the year. For us kids, it was literally time off for good behavior. When Christmas was on, not even Dad could take the joy out of the holidays. Mom did a nice job of meeting everybody's wants but we mostly never even knew what we wanted because we had no idea of what was possible. I got skis once that were probably the last of what was popular before step - in bindings. They were wood with metal edges that were actually screwed to the bottoms. The poles were made of bamboo and leather, the whole package only slightly used. One year, I got a new wheelbarrow for cleaning out horse stalls, but I had actually *asked for it!* Later on, the twins would get new hoes for Christmas – Dad's idea of a joke. But those hoes got pretty well worn out just the same.

We'd all troupe down to Gramp's house on Christmas Eve just as soon as we knew we wouldn't be in the way. Mom was always there from the middle of the afternoon, helping Gram put the spread together. I'd find Gramp and lug in some firewood and then campaign to start the fire that would be the center of my world throughout the evening. It was a great fireplace that lit up the whole room as Gramp held court with whoever wanted to chat. When we got older and started putting together concoctions from behind the bar, Gramp started watching the bottle of Old Overholt that had probably been there since before I was born. One year, me and David (who used to be Shorty) and the cousins all took shots off of that bottle and then Gramp took it away and poured it down the sink.

I played "Silver Bells" for Mom every year I ever had a horn and now I have two. Mom would just melt when she heard it, like it was all she ever wanted for Christmas. I don't know how she ever put a Christmas together for five kids on truck driver's pay but Mom was pretty good at frugal. In those days, the Yankee thrift that made us save the ribbons and the unmolested wrapping paper was probably the very reason we were able to enjoy Christmas morning as we did. Mom didn't celebrate whatever she got from Dad, and Dad always got socks and underwear. We'd pool our money to get Mom something nice and Dad something practical. One year we got Mom a nice AM-FM radio for the kitchen that would also run on batteries. She was overwhelmed, and it turned her into a Red Sox fan. For us, it meant that she'd be sure to hear the school closings on snowy days.

We'd wipe out Christmas morning and then we'd have to go to church. Even Dad wouldn't try to get out of it, both Christmas and Easter. Mom used to say that Dad had more than enough religion without going to church. Dad would say that he'd had enough of religion, period. He just left Mom to explain his absence but when he did go, he was solemn and silent at Mass and us kids were always especially aware of ourselves. Eleven o'clock was "high Mass" and being the last one, it had potential to go on for a whole lot longer than it needed to. We never went to high Mass.

Gramp was a Christmas baby, born in December as was Gram – a year and a day apart. Gramp always put up Christmas lights and I could help as soon as I was old enough. The first year Gramp decided not to put up his lights was the year before he died and me and David did it for him. When we took the lights down in the spring, Gramp gave me the whole set. They still had some life left in them so we started decorating a huge blue spruce tree in our front yard. I'd string the lights with a long pole for as high as I could reach and not even make it half way. Then Peter Pan and Joe Flats would come by with Ladder 1 so I could dress the tree the rest of the way up. The last year of that came as another firefighter got caught "misappropriating city property" when a neighbor turned him in. All he did was stop off at his house for a moment with Engine 2 and he almost lost his job. So now there would be no more misappropriating Ladder 1 and we had to leave Gramp's lights in the tree until the hurricane took it, but they lasted two more years.

Christmas Eve at Gram&Gramp's ended the year Mom died. It happened about the middle of December and aside for what needed to be done for the kids, nobody was in any mood to celebrate. It was like when Great Gramma died when we were kids except that now we had our own, so we went through the motions like our parents must have. I played "Silver Bells" for Mom and I strung more lights for Gramp, as I have ever since.

FIGHTN'

Aside from being a cowboy, I also got caught up in the sweet science of fisticuffs. And Champeen Wrestling. Bobo Brazil, Gorilla Monsoon, Bruno Sammartino, Haystacks Calhoon; they were the original non-steroidal ring warriors of their time on black and white television. They spawned the rivalries between the good guys like Pedro Morales, Chief Jay Strongbow, and Andre the Giant against the likes of Freddie Blasie and whoever was in Lou Albano's stable. Anybody who used to watch this nonsense would remember Freddie Blasie for his famous "heart punch" and how he used to file his teeth on camera. Professor Turo Tanaka and Mr. Fuji were the tag team villains who even got to win once in a while. Then Vince McMahon (who used to be that skinny, deferential milquetoast on the ringside microphone) discovered what this sideshow could really become and he did a masterful job of promoting the sport. When Hulk Hogan appeared, that was the end of porky guys throwing each other around the ring. Didn't matter how popular they were.

I followed boxing too, but I could never tell you who anybody was at the time because the TV was always fuzzy and I was too young to care. We watched for the knock-out like we watched NASCAR for the crashes. Dad got us boxing gloves once but we were old enough to hurt each other and Dad wouldn't ever even watch us fight. Mom only said something about it once and then the boxing gloves disappeared. We were left to argue about who had lost one pair of boxing gloves until the other pair didn't matter and they too were soon gone. We had good football helmets. Mine was just like YA Tittle's because Kevin Barney said he was the greatest quarterback ever. Since I didn't know the names of any other quarterbacks, I could only agree. Gram might have paid for the helmets because she was so afraid we'd get a concussion. Or maybe not wake up at all. Her worst fear for us was that we'd end up in an Iron Lung. Sometimes football games with the cousins would turn into a back yard war where we should have had the boxing gloves. Whacking a pretty good football helmet barehanded was like hitting a brick.

Dad was the toughest kid in his school and the toughest kid in Meshanticut and we wanted to be just like Dad. And in return, wouldn't Dad be proud of us being just like him! I grew up lying in wait for someone to give me good reason to go off so I could prove myself. It didn't really change until suddenly everybody around me was a lot bigger than I was, then I got to be a little more selective. But up until that time, I was just fearless. I took on two of the Twogae brothers at once right where the nuns crossed from the convent to the school. I took on a kid twice my size because he was picking on my sister. Drew blood on him; made sure Dad knew.

In seventh grade, I read everything there was about Charles Atlas and Joe Weider. Jack LaLanne was the cardiovascular guy but he was all about the women. We had an all male assembly once in the gym at Cranston West High School and a muscled - up body builder by the name of Bruce Randolf offered a seminar and a demonstration of what we all could be like. When he snatched a 110 pound barbell clear overhead with one hand and in one motion, I was hooked. Mr. Lemoi started a body - building club that would work out every day after school and I was there whenever I could finagle a ride home. I weighed 114 pounds and I got to where I could bench press 120 and I looked it - at least in the mirror. Julie Moreau never seemed to notice.

I didn't fight a lot in junior high school; I didn't feel like I had a whole lot left to prove. I wasn't mad at anyone and besides, fights took place after school and "over the hill". This was always a show and always drew a crowd, especially when the girls fought but I'd have to miss the bus and it was a two and a half mile walk home if no one was headed that way. Too bad I couldn't ride my horse to school like on TV but they must have known that I would have ridden right past the high school and followed my Boy Scout compass west. If I did show up at school I would have hobbled my horse out on the football field and all the girls would love me because girls love horses. He was actually my second horse since Lucky got old; a black and white quarter horse who was a prime mover. But I had to give up being a cowboy for the next thirty years or so because life and Algebra were closing in fast. I came home from school one day and the horse was gone and so was Dad – driving long - haul for Johnson Motor Lines for days at a time now. I was devastated and so was Mom.

Mom's new living hell worked out for me but only because there was no one at home to push me around. I was the oldest and I rode herd on the others and Mom knew she could take to her bed for a little private decomposure as long as I was around. Except for Boy Scout meetings, my life was about Algebra and Latin and smoking in the tree fort and MAD magazine. We'd still get together with the cousins for that, especially if I managed to swipe a new girlie magazine from old Shadrack down the street. He knew about it, too – probably gave him a chuckle. He kept them stacked in the corner of his garage right near the door and it was an easy caper. I'd also grab a whole pack of "weeds" from Mom because even when she missed it, she'd blame Dad. If they thought we were smoking, they never let on because really, what are a couple of heavy smokers going to say to their kids about smoking? One of our worst tragedies ever was when a storm invaded the tree fort and soaked all the cigarettes and all the magazines.

Academically, it was a terrible time. Instead of being the celebrated genius, I got it from all sides about my need to apply myself so that I could get into one of the best colleges. I missed my horse terribly and there still wasn't Julie Moreau or Carol Pastore and all I could do now was study. I used to drop in on Gram a lot just to talk but she was always on about the drug pushers on every corner just waiting to grab me up and get me addicted, so after a while I stayed away from there, too. I lived at my desk in my room while life went on around me and I never got better than a C minus in Algebra that year. I had to repeat Latin One the following year before I could qualify for Latin Two but lovely Miss Cobb got me through it because I did an excellent job of mowing her lawn and she liked me. Then she encouraged me not to take Latin Three unless I was willing to translate Virgil and Cicero.

I wasn't really all that stupid, though. In sixth grade everybody took an aptitude test so they would be able to place you with like kind in junior high school. They would assign your new seventh grade division a letter of the alphabet and there would be enough letters to make up a word. Once the word got figured out, you knew where you had placed. The genius wiz kids were in "D", next came "E" and on until we had spelled out:

DEMOCRATS

The "D" kids were in accelerated everything, assigned to the most braniac teachers. "E" and "M" kids were considered bright enough to excel with average instruction and the kids near the end of the word were headed for general education or shop class. I was assigned to the "E" division and the expectations never let up. As it happened, my first Algebra teacher was denied tenure due to terminal incompetence and his replacement went on to require some psychiatric evaluation and then disappeared also. So I guess it wasn't just me.

The first few divisions of seventh grade offered students the opportunity to select a foreign language. The whole first half of that school year was devoted to three weeks each of Spanish, French, Italian, or Latin. At the end you would select your interest and have a second choice just it case. I selected French and Dad selected Latin which I had paid no attention to during those three weeks because I knew I'd be taking French. Someone told Dad that you had to have Latin to get into college – any college – and he wasn't going to hear otherwise and I would be taking Latin. Miss Cobb picked up Latin class right where she had left off but that was weeks ago when I was still riding with Roy Rogers or the Cisco Kid. I was kinda screwed because she certainly wasn't about to teach it all over again and I never caught up.

Gym class taught us that all men aren't really created equal and that we were all in various stages of pubescent development. Boys and girls were strictly segregated for gym class and there were only a few of us who had any idea of what the girl's locker room even looked like. There were gang showers that were required and no escape from nakedness. There was swimming at the Gladstone Street School – again, strictly segregated – where Mr. Lynch impressed upon us that we were indeed "all made of the same stuff". I thank him for that and for all of his other kindness to a confused and misinformed adolescent crowd. Mr. Lynch was a celebrated athlete in his day; won quite a lot at swimming. He coached some Olympic prospects while at the same time, he got a lot of kids over their fear of deep water.

Along with junior high school came dancing lessons - ballroom no less. Every mother of the time would insist that their sons and daughters endure the embarrassment of connecting politely with the opposite gender. There would be no escape - not for me nor the cousins - jacket and tie required. Mr. and Mrs. Stetson taught the program two evenings a week at the high school where boys were required to ask politely and girls could not refuse. Poor Carole Pastore became my captive in those days and her appreciation of my affection was somewhat less than apparent. Undeterred, I would always ask for her hand anyway. She was so pretty.

On the home front, Dad always slept or headed out to parts unknown. He wasn't hustling at landscaping or welding any more because the long haul money was so good. We never knew where he went and couldn't have cared less except that Mom was tumbling headlong into a terminal abyss. The green medicine wasn't working any more and now she truly hated my sister who at the time, was just trying to get by. Side by side at the kitchen sink, Mom would pick a fight that would lead to blows if I didn't step in to dismiss one of them. One time, me and Shorty hid on the stairway and taped the exchange on the little recorder he got for Christmas that year and played it back for Dad. He and Mom had a very private discussion about this new threat to Dad's freedom and it was decided that I would do the evening dishes alone. This happened right around when Jazzy clocked Mom, who didn't get up right away.

When I was about 12, we were introduced to dentistry. The Teamster's Union had gotten family dental coverage so we all got herded off to see a guy Mom knew in high school. He was big and strong like Dad but his hands could work your mouth quite diligently just the same. He would quite enjoy his time with Mom sitting in attendance, but us kids were just cattle. There was no introduction to any of the procedure; rather, it just began and you had to pay close attention and be very afraid. Novacaine was a two dollar option and Dad wouldn't pay for it. He had had all of his uppers taken out in one sitting and all of his lowers about two weeks later. We made a real mission of staying away from Dad for a while and we never really connected his pain with our new dentist until he started drilling without the Novacaine. Later Mom would tell us about how the Novacaine was delivered straight into your gums with a needle, so it got to where we couldn't argue for or against the pain. Everything to do with that dentist hurt and I went to the guy's funeral just to see him dead.

Life wasn't all bad all the time. We got into boating with that first plywood hull that Dad named after Jazzy. It had a 1958 Johnson 35 on the stern that Dad steered by its' tiller arm. It would pull me up on water-skis because I was so light but anybody bigger had to get up behind the Smith's little cruiser that was much faster. Pretty soon I could slalom, and Dad thought it great fun to set me down in a school of jellyfish. Then he'd whack the throttle to see if I was paying attention; David said so. We got a 21′ Owens cruiser but it was boring and you couldn't ski off of it. We had to tow a dinghy so we could ferry Mom ashore at Goddard Park Beach where she preferred to remain. Mom didn't like the boats at all and if Dad headed out of Greenwich Bay, she'd go below and shake. Mom didn't swim.

The year I started driving, Dad bought a 21′ ChrisCraft that was an open boat and could do about 25 knots. I hadn't been out in it yet but I had imagined for myself a very fine summer before Dad sunk it. It seems that he was the only one who didn't know about the sunken piling just off the shoreline of Warwick Country Club. The piling came through the bottom of the boat and almost rolled the motor onto a couple of guys sitting in the stern. Nobody got hurt, and it's how we came to know Nick the Pirate who had a salvage dragger for people just like Dad. Nick plucked the boat off of the piling and they brought the motor home and Dad's pal Mud Duck got it running while it was still propped up in the back of the truck. Uncle Bob spent a couple of weekends rebuilding the bottom and then that boat got sold as soon as it was done. That was the end of the family boating experience.

Mud Duck put in a swimming pool that we all helped with. They lived way out in Foster where the snow got really deep, but almost every summer weekend, we'd be in that pool. It was at Mud Duck's pool that I first met Ellen, along with a whole slew of other girls that hung out with Mud Duck's daughters. Some times there would be one or more of the girls who hung out near the pool but wouldn't go in. I never gave it a thought but Dad once called me over for a private conversation that began with:

> "I don't know what you know about sex and all,
> but there's times when girls can't go in the pool..."

And that was all there ever was.

The happiest times Mom and Dad ever shared would have been when they were in the "Hilltoppers" square dance club and Mom had something to look forward to on Saturday nights. There was that and house parties and card games with their friends and all of it affordable because nobody had any real money. They had made some other friends in the square dance club besides those that we grew up knowing and this went on for a few years. Nancy used to be our sitter but she got to be beautiful and moved on, probably because Dad was hitting on her. Joanne was next until I got to be old enough to do it for free. Then it seemed like they were always gone and I was always in charge. I guess I got a good enough allowance for it, but a dollar a week didn't go very far and sometimes I didn't always get it. My authority was absolute. I could make everybody go to bed so I could sit and watch TV alone with a bowl of potato chips like Mom did. Nothing exciting ever happened on my watch and Laddie would have handled any burglar who came by, anyway. Besides, I knew where the shotgun was and I'd have used it, too, just like that kid down south that saved his whole family. *Saved his family* - the fantasy of every eldest son. Some criminal named Hollenbaugh had the mother and the father tied up in the kitchen and this kid poked a 12 gauge through the window and blew Hollenbaugh's brains out with a 12 gauge deer slug. Bet his dad was proud of him!

Not mine, though, and me with no idea of what it would take. I played football in ninth grade in a pre – high school league called CLCF. Cranston Leagues for Cranston's Future. Ninth grade is the last stop in this league before high school and almost everybody in it had been playing since early childhood. I had a lot of catching up to do if I ever wanted to play for real because some of these kids were really good and any newcomer my size would have to show that he wouldn't get killed out there. I had a few shining moments at defense but as a running back I went nowhere. I played zero quarters of high school football and only a few at junior varsity. Dad came to most games and left with nothing to brag about while I sat the bench for three years. Whether Dad did that for me or just because he felt obligated is a judgment call because Dad never spoke about it and I wasn't about to ask. At the end he marched in and yelled at the coach for treating me like Dad didn't matter.

I dated a cheerleader from our school, a cheerleader from another school and a girl from our arch-rival in West Warwick – all of them consecutively. I went 0 for 3 with all of them. What I knew about girls from the outset was that guys went with girls like in the Archie comics and someday they got married. My first date was a movie with Joan Mullins, right after I got my driver's license. She was a nice girl and it was her first date also and we both knew how to act appropriately and I don't know why we didn't date again. There was another part of me longing for what girls are *really* supposed to be about but initially, the Catholic Boy Scout in me almost never made a move. Besides, nobody I knew was prepared for any of *that.* If I tried to get anywhere past the creative kissing stuff, I'd find myself alone again. There were guys bragging about some of what they did and *to whom* and when it got back to the offended party, they found themselves to be alone also. Once, in ninth grade English Miss Lorenzo intercepted a note between two of the more libidinous girls in class. They were quite embarrassed and Miss Lorenzo was visibly shaken by what she had read and these two girls got a really good talking to later. Miss Lorenzo always took an interest in saving some of us from ourselves. She was pretty savvy - should have been a guidance counselor.

Speaking of which, guidance counselors were supposed to be just that -professionals who could nurture a class in general or an individual in particular. Point you in the right direction, as it were. When it came time, you were supposed to politely ask your assigned counselor for a written recommendation for college admission and your guidance counselor was supposed to graciously respond in kind. Maybe if you didn't have the grades or weren't an Eagle Scout, this letter from your guidance counselor might get you in. When I approached Mrs. Trombi for mine, she screeched right into my face:

"NOT FROM ME WILL YOU EVER, EVER, GET A RECOMMEND!!!

"Huh?"

"YOU HEARD ME!! NOT FROM ME!! GET SOMEBODY ELSE!! IF ANYBODY DOESN'T DESERVE TO GO TO COLLEGE, IT'S YOU!!!"

"But I took a college prep program! What should I do?"

"I DON'T CARE IF YOU DIG IN A DITCH!!!
Then she stalked away.

I have no idea to this very day of what that was about. Mr. Leonard saw the whole thing and he had no idea, either. After she was gone, he offered to write my college recommend because he had been my counselor the previous year and we had always been fine with each other - an argument for continuity if ever there was one.

Boy Scouts

My greatest influence from about sixth grade on was the Boy Scouts of America. I was introduced to a whole new world of freedom and adventures that have lent themselves over the years to the creation of my center. God, country, duty, integrity – these were the values that a post-WWII America wanted to instill in its' offspring, perhaps for the next war. The Boy Scouts carried that banner and echoed that spirit resoundingly. There was spit and polish and discipline aplenty if you took it seriously enough and I bought into all of it. Too bad there was no place for Boy Scouts on my report card. I excelled at being a Boy Scout and for a while I was the youngest Eagle Scout that Troop Six Cranston or the State of Rhode Island had ever produced. My Eagle Scout board of review took place about a week after I became eligible and I prepared for it way beyond the necessary; took none of it for granted. My Eagle Scout cut me a lot of breaks. I know it got me into college because my SAT's didn't and it was also mentioned at my hiring interview for the real fire department. Eagle Scout helped others get into the armed forces academies and it has produced some of our more capable leaders. Scouting brought me back from internal exile. The skills that were so important to living in the wild (or just plain living) became second nature and I imagined a life in the woods that few aside from Daniel Boone could envision. If I were born 50 years earlier, I could have been the Eagle Scout Paul Siple who was chosen to accompany Admiral Byrd to Antarctica. This was a world filled with my kind of people, so much so that I really started thinking about building a career around it. Dad could barely acknowledge my Eagle Scout because it wasn't about him or anything he cared about and he'd have to admit that he was almost wrong about me being a nitwit.

For the first time, Dad didn't matter.

Champlin Reservation is the finest piece of real estate I truly hope the developers continue to salivate over – right in the heart of western Cranston. If the Boy Scouts of America look to perpetuate the organization in Rhode Island, they can never lose Camp Yawgoog and they should never lose Champlin. I had the run of Champlin Reservation throughout my Scouting years because the camp ranger and Gramp were fast friends. Arthur Liedman was a true woodsman who knew field and stream and forest his whole life and he was very generous about passing it along. Gramp had built some rustic shelters and some latrines at Champlin and he did a nice job of it and treated the Boy Scouts pretty well about price. Both were good men of their time and they left their print on the likes of myself and of others who were paying attention. There were a few of us who spent a lot of time at Champlin; it was a mile down the road from me and a mile up the road for my friend Steve Hogan and it was like having the run of a wildlife preserve. We climbed shear rock face at TipTop Ledge and we tracked skunk and muskrat and we knew the difference in mud at a glance. We were among the few who could help ourselves to a seat by the woodstove in the ranger's office while Art Liedman and Art Chew talked about the future of the place. I was among the first to learn that Champlin Reservation would soon own a massive tract across Scituate Avenue that would double the size of the camp. Old man Helgersen had been in talks with the Boy Scouts for a while and he didn't need the money and he didn't like developers. They tunneled under Scituate Avenue so we could all safely get to the new property and sometimes there was deer track at both ends.

Camp Yawgoog was the largest Boy Scout camp in the world before they bought Philmont in New Mexico. My first week at Yawgoog was my first week ever away from home and it was awesome. I was eleven years old and Dad wasn't even embarrassed that I still couldn't swim but before that first week was out, I could manage the two laps you needed to qualify as a "beginner". It meant that you could take out a rowboat with somebody else who was at least a beginner as long as you wore life jackets. "Swimmers" – four laps or more – could take out a canoe or a rowboat or a sailboat *all by themselves!* My second year, I qualified as a "swimmer" and every year after at Yawgoog, I made the Mile Swim – even when I was on staff there. It was a fascinating place to spend a week, let alone the entire summer. Troop Six was widely renowned as a competitive camping organization and we didn't have anybody who didn't pull their own weight. The few of us who could embrace the grueling Narragansett Council Honor Hike sneered at the troops who sent kids that would slow us down. We won at almost everything there was (I'm bragging, here) and we always camped in Sandy Beach during Recall Week – the last week of the Yawgoog season, the last week of August. The camp director was H. Cushman "Gus" Anthony and he tooled around camp in a yellow Model T Ford. He was courtly in manner, grandfatherly in appearance, and he was always in charge. I'd work for Mr. Anthony again in an instant.

It was on staff at Yawgoog that I came to learn about what some other adults might have in mind. When I spent the summer of 67' living my dream of working at Camp Yawgoog, some controversies entirely failed to surface that would put people in jail very quickly today. I was 15 and there was no such thing as gay - just queer – and I never really knew anything about the queers, not at school and certainly not in the Boy Scouts. Nobody ever spoke about the queers except maybe to use the term as an insult and no one was calling me a queer. Even if a guy seemed a little faggy, we wouldn't call him a queer unless we thought so for sure. But nobody ever really knew for sure because the queers looked just like the rest of us. Maybe I just wasn't paying enough attention. No such thing as "don't ask; don't tell." either. We didn't know it at the time but the gay/straight ratio has always been pretty much the same wherever you live or eat or worship. They're not all in one place. I'm sure I must have known a few queers back then but "gay-dar" hadn't been invented yet and I mostly didn't care. No one did. Never knew anything about pedophiles either but it came out later that Camp Yawgoog seemed to have more than a few. They weren't exactly wearing badges so it must have been quite an undertaking to ferret them out. Maybe somebody squealed because a scandal caught up with one of the big shot camp administrators and it made it into the newspaper. These afflictions were settled quietly; he just apologized to the court and disappeared. Nobody would admit that such crimes routinely existed or that they had ever been a victim or maybe were even drawn to it. Sickening stuff, that.

There were three divisions at camp: Sandy Beach, Medicine Bow, and Three Point. Seasoned campers of Sandy Beach would point out that Medicine Bow was for rich kid sissies who had to be close to everything and that Three Point was a slum. Any waterfront position was a plum job because those guys lived in their Speedos and slept upstairs in Olympic Village overlooking Yawgoog Pond. They got to water ski off of the power boat in front of all the girls who came with the families on Sunday. No queers there, for sure. Kitchen help was the only staff that got paid that first year because their workload was more demanding. They got $100 for the summer while the rest of us newbies worked for room and board only. It sucked, being kitchen staff (except for the baker's helper) but they were just as happy to be there as anybody. I worked the counter at the Sandy Beach trading post and I filled in for the bugler on his day off. The only reason I ever went home on my day off was to see Laddie, who as Mom reported, missed me terribly. I felt badly about that and I missed him too but a whole summer away from Dad and everybody else was the best break I ever caught. My boss at Camp Yawgoog was this faggoty guy whose parents bought him a brand new Mustang for his birthday at camp, just to keep him from being queer (or maybe just because they really loved him). He acted pretty queer just the same; seems that these guys always find each other. It was *his* boss who tried to get to me with a line that left no doubt about what he was up to. I used to walk the cash box down to the Bucklin administration building near Three Point and I would grab a hot shower while I was there. I was walking back to Sandy Beach when this guy offered me a ride the rest of the way. He was a fat guy who looked like a rodent and there were rumors about him. Secure as I was in my manhood, I just stared out the window at his remark. Besides, if he ever tried anything, I would tune him up pretty good and then Dad would rip out his arm and beat him to death with it and I'd get to watch. So I just got out of the car. That was my first and last experience with anybody like that. We had heard that they were out there but they must be somebody else's problem in another country or something because no one I knew was ever approached except me. How many of "me" he might have gotten to is unknown because it is quite a solo experience. I saw this same guy many years later at a Triple A office and it was all I could do to hold myself back. I told Carolyn I had to go out to the car because what I really wanted to do was to vault the counter and beat this guy bloody, just like Dad would have.

Richard Sharp was in Troop Six with me and we were best friends. He had an uncle who sent home electronic stuff and photo gear from when he was overseas in the service. Richard was a wizard at photography and he also had some of the best stereo equipment around – had cassettes when they first came out. We used to go down to Narragansett Pier and shoot telephoto of bikinis across the water at Scarborough Beach and then we'd go to Scarborough and shoot telephoto at the Pier. We got some great stuff that Richard turned into a wicked cool slideshow. He also had gorgeous twin sisters who were a couple of years younger but they had real potential and one of them once tried me out for a long, slow kiss. I was always welcome at his house and I got to go to their beach house at Sagamore on Cape Cod for summer weekends. I used to play Yahtzee with his mom and I know she thought the world of me until she heard me cuss in my sleep. We fished for "tinker" mackerel and tried to get really lucky with the girls on the beach and we didn't care whose daughters they were. Every summer night was a party on Cape Cod; parents went one way and kids went the other. One night this kid Tom drank most of a fifth of Southern Comfort and we had to watch him real close in case we needed to get him to a hospital. He was older and he got us the liquor so we had to save him or else. Me and Richard and some other guys were headed to Woodstock that summer when Dad figured out that I might not really be going to Cape Cod that weekend and wouldn't let me off of the hill. I heard they had a great time – should have sent me a post card. Dad didn't have much use for "them long haired creepy sons of bitches' that looked like they crawled out from under a rock". No hippies in our house, no sir. We got a whole lot of "my country, right or wrong" crap and when Muhammed Ali refused to be drafted, Dad went right over the top with rage. "Who's that nigger think he is...?" he'd say and that would kick off the whole nigger rant. Heavyweight champion of the world? Dad would take him in a New York minute and make it look easy.

Troop 6 ended when I took my Eagle to be with Troop 33 that one of the uncles had taken over. "A leader of boys, not men" Dad would growl because Dad wasn't a leader of anybody. I wasn't pressured to leave Troop 6 nor was I invited to join Troop 33 but there wasn't room at the top in Troop 6 for me and the assistant scoutmaster's other son. Since I had someplace I could go and he didn't, I asked to transfer out. I sat down with Mr. Curtis the Scoutmaster and asked him if he'd mind.

"It's hard to lose one of your own" he said.

Mr. Curtis was especially good to me but he was especially good to all of us. I always needed a ride home from Boy Scout meetings and one night my ride up Scituate Avenue failed to make it to the meeting. Mr. Curtis said he'd take me home and we'd drop off Louie DiMasi along the way. Louie did a "got you last" on me as he got out of the car and I chased him in and out of his garage. The door was hanging low and it was dark and I ran into the overhang full bore and the blood that came next was unstoppable. Mr. Curtis harrumphed a little, took me all the way home to pick up Mom, and then all the way over to Dr. Donahue's house for stitches. Dr. Donahue was on his back under a '58 Chevy wagon putting in a clutch and now it was almost ten o'clock. There would be no "Hi-ya Handsome" from Dr. Donahue tonight.

How any of us ever made it through childhood could only be explained by a higher power since we seemed to be up for any adventure that would get us killed. My career on the rescue truck brought me face to face with the consequences of bad luck or poor timing and the fact that I should never have survived my teen years. We had a lot of opportunity and sometimes I think that Dad must have had us all insured for more than the cost of burial, because we were handed guns and cars and bows and arrows in our early years with no adult supervision whatsoever. We used to shoot real arrows across the bedroom into a wicker clothes hamper that stood against the wall but we quit that when we discovered that the arrows were coming out the other side and chipping the wall. One time we shot some out the open window and we missed picking one up and Dad found it and took the bow away for a while. We had a neat way of re-charging D cell batteries. We'd wire them to an electric train transformer for an hour or so and they'd be good as new but not for very long. One time, we left one cooking while we went to church and came home to find that the battery had exploded and left a dark stain on the ceiling. We washed off the worst of it as best we could and rubbed some baby powder into it to minimize the blemish. They never knew, or just never asked. Dad didn't come upstairs often and when he did, it was because someone namely me was in deep trouble. One time, I got into it with Mom over something and she heard the "...what a bitch" part I didn't know I had said. Its' a continuing problem – sometimes when I think, my lips move. When Dad got home, he made a point of one step at a time so we could count the seconds to my doom, David being a material witness and all. Dad filled the doorway with dread and his glare actually gave off heat:

"Got something to say about your mother?"

I couldn't make myself small enough and David who was my brother and best friend and roommate suddenly made himself invisible. There was no escape and nothing I could say that would save me this time so I looked right at him and clamped down on my bladder. I should have said a quick "Hail Mary" while he was still on the stairs.

"She never quits and you're never here."

He glared at me for about another hour or maybe just a few seconds and abruptly turned and left. Me and David just looked at each other, as in "Huh?". Then Dad and Mom had another private discussion about this latest threat to Dad's freedom so Mom would leave us alone.

I learned to drive at about eleven and it was a total set-up. Dad had a 1959 Ford four wheel drive that he plowed snow with and he knew I was dying to drive, just like the cousins next door. We were all around the same age but Uncle Bob next door used to restore Model A Fords and his two sons were ace mechanics and I wasn't. Dad being a truck driver and all, it wouldn't look too good if someone else taught his kids to drive so he made it work for him. Our gravel driveway was only a single car wide - no garage. Dad wanted it double wide and soon enough I was learning a four-speed. I shook like a leaf next to Dad, trying so hard not to pop the clutch and stall the truck. But me and David would have dug him a parking lot just for the opportunity to drive the dirt off. Later on we got a '52 Chevrolet from old Mrs. Smith that had a rod knock but the car was otherwise perfect. Dad said that we'd pull the oil pan and shim the rod but instead, someone gave Dad $25 for it. Meanwhile, the cousins were running a cut down Model A tractor through Gramp's woods while we had to wait for something else. One after another, we killed off woods cars. We almost got asphyxiated in a Renault Dauphine that burned more oil than gas and David had a '56 Chevy until Jazzy kissed a tree with it and loosened her front teeth. Then we banged out the damage and kept right on destroying that car. We got a '48 Crosley Hot Shot that had its' clutch disc frozen to the flywheel. A bunch of us hoisted the car up on its' side while Dad's pal Mud Duck freed up the clutch. We ran that car through the woods where it used to get stuck all the time because it only had twelve inch wheels, but two of us could almost always push it out. The Crosley was made by the same company that was famous for refrigerators but they were only in the car business for a few years. The car had an overhead cam four cylinder and it was way ahead of it's time by Detroit standards so it didn't sell too well. None of the little cars did except maybe for Volkswagon but they had their own following and it didn't have anything to do with V-8 power. I had designs on putting that Crosley on the road when I was old enough but Dad cut it down to make a garden tractor. All he did was ruin it, so Mud Duck took it to power a saw rig. But it was the Oldsmobile and the Model A cut-down that almost got us killed time and again.

Long before we could drive, we had Gramp's woods and the neighboring wilderness all scoped out. Gramp had kept the rest of his property undeveloped and we always had free run of it and Dad never bothered us. The old wagon roads from colonial times went on for miles, intersected by stone walls and new growth. We'd leave Gramp's woods and hike over property that was once a part of the original Lawton Farm on Plainfield Pike, where two elderly sisters worked the land long after their husbands had died.

It had the neatest old barn from the early eighteen hundreds that accidentally burned down to make way for industrial development in 1970. I got the worst case of poison ivy ever from digging in the farm dump in the early spring, just before the leaves would emerge. We got some neat old bottles and some other ancient debris for our trouble. After they carted the old women away and the farm was abandoned, we'd explore the place and pick the Concord grapes so Mom could make a winter's supply of jam. There was an old Dodge pickup with a tree growing through it right at the edge of Henry's farm where we used to steal pumpkins. I grabbed some parts off it years ago for the truck I run today.

Parked at the edge of the woods were a couple of original Fordson tractors that Gramp used to pull stumps with but they hadn't run for years and the motors were frozen. One of these tractors had regular front end steering but with tracks on the rear. Worth a fortune today, it got sold for scrap. The other sat until we decided that we might be able to break the motor free by dragging it through the woods with the cousins' Model A cut-down. Now this Model A cut-down was a whole lot more than just a Model A Ford with the fenders cut away. This beast had the original Ford front end and power train, but it also had an auxiliary four speed and a big – assed truck differential with tires like off of a semi. In double high it could probably do a very scary 45 or so but in double low, it would pull a train. We got about 20 feet of chain and hooked on to the old tractor and start dragging it through the woods. The big back tires on the Fordson were flatter than flat – spread out over the ground like they had melted in place. Didn't matter a whit; we all hopped on anyway. David sat astraddle the flathead motor and I was perched proudly on the very front atop the radiator, holding on to the cast iron cap. The plan was to drag this thing through the woods in double low - *not too fast* - until something gave. The guys on the cut-down towing us thought we could go a little faster and about halfway up the track, we really got rolling. The flat tires on the Fordson got out of step with each other and we went completely out of control when this giant pair of conjoined oak trees was headed right at me. I bailed out at the last moment and hit the dirt but David never had time to get off. When the Fordson hit the trees the front end broke into pieces and curled the hand crank a bit. David got a spark plug in the cheek of his ass that should have gotten stitches and a tetanus shot but we ran home and patched up the hole and washed the blood out of his underwear. For all of our time and trouble, that motor didn't loosen one bit. We dragged it back to where we had found it and tried to think up a reasonable explanation in case anybody ever asked. About a year later, Dad asked Gramp if he could scrap that old tractor and then he asked the cousins to drag it out with the cut-down. No one spoke a word as Dad examined the Fordson. And then he didn't want to know what happened:

> "Gets pretty cold up here, eh? Look at how the cold must've busted that cast. Frozen in time, ha, ha."

We just looked at each other as that bullet sped by.

The road through the woods wasn't without obstacles and it certainly wasn't meant for the speeds we imagined. It began where Charcalee Drive ended (where the Fordson was parked) and ran for about a half mile where we made this loop around a giant white pine. Our very first challenge was a big rock that jutted up through the very middle of the road. It wouldn't have bothered horse and wagon at all, but it certainly would take out an oil pan so it had to go. We dug for weeks, finally exposing a piece of granite the size of the cars we were driving. The glaciers were very generous to New England and there is big rock everywhere so this one was no surprise. Our solution was to dig a deep hole and simply push it in. We dug all the way around and *under* this monstrosity and then we cut down a tree that was big enough to use as a lever. Four of us bouncing on the end of it made it wiggle a little but we needed more weight and it had to go in one motion so we had to go and get Dad and Uncle Bob. When they came up to see what we had done, you could tell they were pretty impressed but they didn't say much. They just kept looking at how we had tunneled under that rock. When the stone finally tumbled into the hole, it still stuck up a couple of inches but it was right in the middle of the road and it never bothered us again. We never built a lot of extra road in Gramp's woods, just enough to turn around in. We'd have had to cut down too many trees and trees leave stumps and stumps don't come out too easily and they ruin tires. We were happy enough with what we had and we could get up some pretty good speed. Drove like madmen, actually. I had a '57 Oldsmobile that somebody gave us because the front end needed rebuilding. Aside from that, the car was immaculate and ran really well. It had a 371 with a four barrel carburetor and we cut quite a lot off of the car to lighten it up a little. The front bumper alone must have weighed 200 pounds. David had one of those square Ramblers from the 50's that you couldn't kill and the cousins had the cut-down. Funny how you could always tell a Rambler driver in those days; they always just poked along, leading a whole line of cars anxious to pass. Nowadays they drive Buicks. This is no reflection on David because he drove as crazy as the rest of us. I was just sayin'.

I could do a lot with that Oldsmobile. I could start at one end of the track and stick my foot in it all the way up to "the pines" where you had to make the loop around the biggest tree. The Olds couldn't make it in one turn because it was too long and didn't have enough steering radius. The track was only one car wide so I learned to take the Olds into a four point slide so I could go right around that tree and head straight out; didn't want to hold anybody up. Every so often though, all the gas would shift to one side of the carburetor and the Olds would stall. It happened once with the cut-down chasing me and I couldn't get a re-start. He came at me broadside thinking he'd stop just short and scare the hell out of me except that the mechanical brakes on the cut-down failed and he drove the channel ends of the cut-down frame right through where I was sitting. I had sense enough to spring over to the other side of the Olds just as the cut-down sliced into us but it scared me plenty just the same. It was a pretty good hit – moved the Olds sideways a foot or so. Dad saw the hole and fashioned a bumper across the front of the cut-down with no mention at all about the only way this could have happened. Must've had us insured, I swear.

We were pretty close to driving age when we got the dune buggy. That's what we called it. Actually, it was this old Chrysler frame with an engine and a seat that we bought off of Kenny Andrew. It had a 354 wedge with a push-button automatic transmission and it's a good thing it only had a two barrel carburator because it was plenty dangerous enough. It had short straight manifold pipes dumping flame out of each side and a couple of tubular school bus seats gas welded to the frame. The fuel supply was a two gallon oil can mounted on the very front of the frame on a cross member. We used to wind it up right in front of the house, punch the "drive" button, and try to get the front end to come up off of the street. It had no brake pedal so you would have to pull on the emergency brake that grabbed onto part of the drive line to slow it down enough so that you could punch "reverse" to stop. If you didn't do it in that order or you missed "reverse" then you couldn't stop until you hit something. I drove this death defying machine up the track one time and launched it into a four point slide around the tree just because I could and the seat gave way from under me. My ass fell into the emergency brake friction plate which was red hot from use and I had to hold myself up by the steering wheel or else fall through the frame and run myself over. We stopped when we hit another tree that busted off the gas tank but it failed to ignite. Clearly, modifications were in order.

We stole gas anywhere and everywhere and no one was safe except our dads. Others - neighbors, people down the road – any place we could sneak up to or under somebody else's car was fair game. We got to a Caddy that was visiting another uncle that was always good for ten gallons or so but we over-reached a little once and we got some second hand flak about it. There was a Mafia guy up the road who always had a collection of visiting Cadillacs at his house. We only wanted to hit them for five gallons at a time which wouldn't really be missed in a Caddy but that also meant too many trips to the well. If we ever got caught, we'd surely disappear, but still... Once, we crept up to a long abandoned Plymouth in back of Wolanski's house where I passed out cold after I lost suction and took in a load of stale fumes. No one knew what to do so they decided that we'd stay there until I either woke up or was judged to be dead. No one had a better plan, so it's a good thing I woke up. We never got caught and no one ever questioned where we got our gas from – at least not to us. We never stole from Gramp, either, except for cigars.

The first of us to drive – me'n older cousin – had to take driving lessons behind the wheel. We were pretty insulted since we'd been driving for years now but it was for a big insurance discount. We had to go out with this fat guy Vinny from the driving school for an hour lesson that he slept through. An hour from Cranston R.I. will take you past the beaches and into Connecticut so by the time this guy woke up, there was no getting him back in time for his next client. He was none too happy about it and he got me back good later on when he hired me to take a truck load of stones out of his yard. Three loads later, he wouldn't pay the bill and there was nothing legal I could do about it so I got some gas off of him, too. And his wife. And the Caddy next door.

The drivin' years pretty much cut us loose. We quit stealing gas and we junked the woods cars and we were almost never home. Insurance regulations being what they were, we were insured as "part time" drivers at a fraction of what it cost to put a kid in his own car. One of the cousin's other uncles owned an insurance agency and he took pretty good care of all of us. I only had one minor mishap when Billy McGirr almost backed into me and I shoved it in reverse and backed into David Levy's '61 Ford. You couldn't tell my dent from all of the others but Dad settled with his Dad anyway. I was amazed that there wasn't a lot of Dad's usual crap about it but Dad was happy enough that we weren't getting sued and that the insurance wasn't involved. One mishap, no matter how minor, would about double the premiums for a young, single, male driver.

The tree fort didn't matter any more since we could just smoke in the car. Since everybody smoked, we all smelled the same. Mom switched from Chesterfield non-filtered cigarettes to Winston 100's after Arthur Godfry (the famous radio and TV star) got cancer. Dad switched from Camel's to Salem menthol when he wasn't bumming off of Mom. We used to wait until Mom was about half way through a carton and then we'd steal a pack and slide the rest forward so she wouldn't catch on. Whenever she did miss a pack, Mom would just blame Dad and Dad would just blow it off like he did everything else. I had my eye on a carton of Lucky Strike that Gramp kept on a shelf in his office that somebody must have given him. Gramp never smoked cigarettes so I helped us out a bit by swiping those Lucky's one pack at a time when we didn't have any in the tree fort. Years later, I was sitting with Gramp when I reached up for the empty carton and tipped it into his lap and the one remaining pack fell out.

I thought I'd get killed if I ever got caught smoking. I used to snatch a cigar out of Gramp's truck once in a while but Mom just thought we spent too much time around Gramp when we reeked of cigar. Twenty years after Gramp died, the Caddy still smelled of cigar. Gram hated it - thought it vulgar and wouldn't let him smoke if she was in the car. Gramp smoked a pipe also; it was how you could tell his day was done. He had a collection of fine briar and he bought a special blend of tobacco. I got my first pipe from Gramp, a corncob that I'd smoke all through college and then some. Borkum Riff tobacco was all the rage then but I enjoyed a little Granger, too. Later, I'd put some other stuff in the pipe that Gram would never approve of.

Me and David used to hang out at the Mister Donut, especially when we were supposed to be at church. One evening we were there and I had a Marlboro going when suddenly:

"It's Mr. Orabone!!"

Mr. Orabone was the football coach. He was out of his car and on his way in when I doused the butt in David's coffee. He made his way to the carry - out side of the doughnut shop where he placed his order.

"Hi Mr. Orabone."

"Hi boys – you all behaving?"

"Yes Mr. Orabone"

After he left, I felt relieved that he never saw me smoking but the next day at football practice, I got it full bore:

"Everybody here know Buttsy?..."

Uh Oh...

"Buttsy, Buttsy Larrivee.. thinks he's so smart...
take a lap for us Buttsy – show me you can still run...
in fact, take a couple – I'll say when you can stop."

I spent the whole afternoon taking laps for Mr. Orabone and then he made the whole team take a couple on my behalf at the end of practice. Since only a few of us smoked, I wasn't too popular that day. I got caught smoking for good one day when Dad said:

"Go get me a cigarette".

I headed into the house to bum one from Mom when he stopped me.

"Gimme one of yours."

"Huh?"

You heard me; gimme one of yours."

I was dumbstruck about what to say next so I just walked over to the Barracuda and reached under the seat for the flip-top Marlboros. I just figured that he must have found them once when he took my car. It's not like I was especially careful.

"...because you use the ashtray"

"What?"

"You use the ashtray and I never do."

It was true. One of my pet peeves with him was that he used to drive with his right hand resting on the edge of the bucket seat and the ashes would form a neat little pyramid on the floor. We never spoke of it again, and I smoked wherever and whenever I wanted. Mom grimaced about it once, but there it ended.

I used to get accused of being where I shouldn't with the car but it was never true. I think Dad was just trying to flesh me out or catch me in a lie. I hated one of his cop friends for years because he had allegedly told Dad that I was hanging out where a big drug bust was about to go down. It was all concocted because I never hung out anywhere; never had the time. I was always working or studying or otherwise engaged in high school activities or

Boy Scouts or girl-friends. It seemed like I hardly slept and I never slept late – even when I could. And I was always home within a few minutes of curfew, breaking a few traffic laws in the effort. Dad's 40 minute Sunday drive home from Foster, R.I would take me a whole lot less.

I did have this one fantasy road trip all planned out in my head. I played in our concert orchestra and I went from trumpet to baritone horn to E-flat mellaphone. The mellaphone sounded just like a French horn but it was easier to play. I got all the choice solos because our one French horn player only acted the part and no sound ever came out. Mr. Goding, our director, arranged an exchange concert with Tenafly, New Jersey where we would stay with their kids and then they would come to stay with us. It was a very ritzy neighborhood and I stayed with the Wood family – a mom and her two sons. It was in Tenafly where I met Jeanne Byler who loved me at first sight and I learned to kiss accordingly. Her dad seemed happy enough that I'd be leaving in a couple of days, but we made the most of every minute together without removing any clothing. I vowed to return and we exchanged letters all winter. I would stay at the Clinton Hotel and no one would ever need to know and we would do this until we could be together forever. None of this ever happened and my first visit to Tenafly, New Jersey would turn out to be my last. Besides, if I ever left Rhode Island on my own at that time, I would have turned west and just kept on going.

What a Jolly Street

Gramp and his business partner, Dick Chartrand were very successful building contractors who had bought a tract of land on a hill off of Scituate Avenue back in the 50's when western Cranston was rural. They pushed a road down the middle, they each took a half, and Mom had the city name it for the three families:

CHARtrand, CAito, and LarrivEE

Hence, Charcalee Drive. As each of his children married, Gramp carved off a house lot as a wedding gift that was almost an acre apiece - one behind the other - where they all built new houses at near cost. Gramp had built a custom ranch at the head of the street on our side and Chartrand did the same on the other. Dads worked, Moms all stayed home, and Gram tried to dictate the terms of how everybody should be raising their kids in this little kingdom Gramp had created for us.

We used to call Dick Chartrand "Uncle Dick" and his wife was "Aunt Frances" just because someone thought they should have a title even though we weren't related. The Chartrands always took special pleasure when any of us Larrivee kids dropped by to amuse them and we were always welcome. We were a personable lot to anyone who would have us because any place was better than home. The next door cousins weren't allowed over there at all because their mom thought that Gramp should just kick his partner to the curb in favor of her husband who happened to be the oldest son. Those lines were clearly drawn early on but other parameters were intentionally vague, especially about the future of "Caito & Chartrand" as " Contractors & Builders". As it played out, Gramp kept his partner at full salary long after he had become too sick to work, almost until he died. Then Gramp put his own name on the business until he retired and then the sons went separate ways. Because we all had to live as neighbors *and* as relatives, a lot didn't get said except for when it did. Then there would be cold war for a while.

"What a Jolly Street" was a neighborhood in a book of fantasy that Jazzy would inhabit for all of her childhood. It was a collection of short stories about a magical place where mothers loved their children and everybody got along like on TV. It was a pretty thick book and I read some of it until I about wanted to throw up, but for Jazzy it was escape from a world that was far and away worse than mine. Mom and Gram so doted on her - indeed nagged her to distraction about every little thing- that Jazzy could never really focus. Rural as we were, Jazzy only had a couple of friends nearby. One was Paula Gooley whose mother was very close to Mom. When the Gooleys' moved out of state, Mom and Jazzy both suffered a tragic personal loss that failed to make them any closer. Life for Jazzy got to be almost entirely about piano and Mom and Gram, who, taken together acted like very old women. Gram had been brought up quite properly through the remnants of the Victorian era and they tried to drag Jazzy back into it. Dad paid no attention whatsoever, except to criticize.

I try to imagine how I could have been more help to Jazzy during that time but I was always paladin to my sister. It wasn't like she couldn't stand for herself, but more like she was individually overwhelmed by the rejection that we both had come to know. We tagged David as the favorite since Mom was always ragging on Jazzy and Dad always had it in for me. While me and Jazzy always took turns at the whipping post, David almost never got punished for anything and on Saturday mornings, he got to go on errands with Gramp. There's a story that Gram and Mom took Jazzy to a specialist to find out why she seemed so socially inept, but it didn't take an expert to see that Jazzy got a fair amount of abuse and almost no parental direction of any value. We stuck up for Jazzy at every turn, me and David. I clobbered kids that would pick on her – even the cousins if they said too much. We let her ride bikes with us and she was a hell of a gig* pusher but as we all got older and figured out how to at least *appear* to be relatively normal, Jazzy didn't. I tried to keep Mom off of her case and I even tried to get over on Gram about how much the world had changed, just in case she was ever that young.

One time Jazzy almost blew up the house. We had a gas range that used propane and the oven had to be ignited with a match and it had to be done sequentially. You'd turn on the gas and hold a wooden match over the pilot hole and then "whoosh" – the oven would ignite. What you *cannot do* is turn the gas on and then walk away which is exactly what Jazzy did. Minutes later, she struck the match and got herself blown across the kitchen, burnished eyebrows and all. Mom's knick-knacks got scattered and there was some window damage but nobody got hurt and the house didn't burn down. Dad just shook his head and said something about a cow stepping on its' own tit.

While Jazzy took up residence on What a Jolly Street, everybody else was stuck on Charcalee Drive except for Dad. Mom was beside herself with anxiety about wherever Dad was and she mostly took it out on Jazzy. Some of Mom's anxiety would be about the hair-raising episodes in long – haul trucking. Once, a big sheet of ice blew off of the rag-top in front of Dad and it hit the windshield dead on. Dad survived because it was a divided windshield that had a bar of steel down the middle. But except for when he was either driving or sleeping, nobody ever knew just where the hell Dad was. I finally had to come in off the range for good and pay more attention at the ranch just to keep order.

Jazzy had joined up with the U.S. Army about a year out of high school. Dad conned her into it - out of sight, out of mind, for everyone. She went in as a clerk and mustered out nine years later as a sergeant clerk and she made little use of her right to a college education. Jazzy had no money, few reliable friends and a baby on the way. She came over one night when she was home on leave to ask about our willingness to commit to the care of her child in the event she was suddenly deployed to a hot zone. Me and Carolyn and David and Suzi all quickly declined to become surrogate parents because too much consideration would have meant that we were actually considering. David and Suzi would soon have their own little bundle of joy and we were all filled up with more than we could manage but we all privately agreed that we'd certainly help Jazzy otherwise. We asked about the father:

" A tall, blonde fellow - mostly German, I think..."

The father would never be a part of the program nor was he tall, blonde, and German unless they somehow make black people from Louisiana that way. Mom was perfectly mortified when she first saw the racing stripe and never recovered. Whatever Dad might have said, he stepped right up to find Jazzy *someplace else* to live. The rest of the family couldn't help but snicker just a little at Dad's good karma, what with him always carrying on like he had.

Jazzy had no formal training in anything other than recital piano. We had always thought that the armed forces offered room, board, and enough of a paycheck to keep a loyal recruit who had nothing else. Nobody had ever imagined Jazzy suddenly back home with child and no longer a soldier. The money that Jazzy had routinely sent home to Mom for safekeeping turned out to be un-founded and Dad would only spend enough to assure a comfortable distance. Mom got as cold as frigid gets, going through the motions of living however she could without throwing up. Jazzy had her baby with the help of complete strangers - all by herself, alone - by choice.

If 95% of life involves just showing up, Jazzy had it all figured out because when she left the army, she showed up for everything

- all the time. It was like she had this route of relatives that she constantly traveled until everybody had someplace else to be or something else to do. The Ford Maverick would pull up without warning and Jazzy would unload the playpen and enough baggage to stay for the day. Then it would be all about you holding and hugging her baby so that Jazzy could enjoy by proxy what she had yearned for all of her life. It was maddening and it was very sad and it was me who had to tell Jazzy that she couldn't just keep showing up all the time without at least a phone call. Then we got dropped from the route.

Jazzy got herself qualified as a CNA* and went to work for an agency where she had way too much to say about the welfare of patients in her care. Details are sketchy, but soon Jazzy found herself out of the CNA business. Had she gone to work for the Veteran's Administration Hospital or the US Postal Service or any other federal government position, Jazzy would already have had nine years in towards a 20 year pension, counting her U.S. Army time. Her military service would have put her at the head of the line and they would have been happy to have such a dedicated employee. Or a city job - where I might have been able to call in a favor or ask one on her behalf. Forever the independent and loyal to a fault, no one ever accused Jazzy of taking good advice. She opted instead to keep a part-time position as assistant manager of the fish market at a local grocery chain. They were going to offer her full time employment with benefits any year now.

I had come to accept that Dad hated the very sight of me but Jazzy would never feel that way about Mom or Dad and she remained loyal, even beyond Mom's tragic end. If Jazzy ever had any idea of some of what Dad used to say about her - about all of us - she might have taken a different view. Even as kids we saw the wrong in that, while Mom and Dad wished for the good in other people's children. Jazzy probably had no idea that she had been disinherited like me and David and after Mom died she wrote odes of sorrow in the newspaper. Loyalty runs deep in Larrivees and Jazzy got more than her share of needing St Jude. Her child failed to become the blessing that Jazzy was expecting and there were police reports and court orders about how the kid failed to behave. Still, Jazzy held her daughter dear while she got to be mostly self-sustaining. Some of us would always rally to keep her $200 problem from becoming a $1000 problem but Jazzy really stood up for herself and her daughter and they made their own way. Dad also had a needy sister who in his words "...would give you the shirt off of somebody else's back". Jazzy isn't like that at all. She'd more likely give you everything she owned.

There wasn't any hand-wringing about the Larrivee's leaving Charcalee Dr. There might even have been a round of applause as they handed over the keys and drove that last load of junk down the road. Dad's collection of crap that he'd always need for something filled more than a couple of 30 yard dumpsters with debris. The rest went to the new farm. Uncle Tom - one of Gramp's brothers - used to visit from time to time. "Junk; nothing but junk..." he'd growl, and he didn't live anywhere near us so you knew he was saying what everyone else was thinking.

When cold war broke out it wasn't always about Dad. Everybody was supposed to abide Gram or at least pay lip service but the people who married in didn't exactly sign off on all of that. The aunts on the hill weren't taking direction from Gram and they made their husbands know it. Then there was "Oak Street" - a collection of Gramp's kin who had remained clustered around GreatGramma for all those years. They were mostly elderly and irrelevant, but that's just because we were only kids when we knew them. Later on, it would become apparent that Gramp helped them out a lot because there was a bit of a fracas about how long that should continue. After GreatGramma ruined Christmas by dying, we pretty much quit going over there. Except for Jazzy, who had put them on her route.

Charcalee Drive would have been a case study for how relatives shouldn't live in clusters. If everybody would just do as Gram said or listened to Gramp whenever he thought it was important, we would have gotten along just fine. But one of the aunts couldn't be told and the other wouldn't be told and Gram's only friend was Mom. Gram was a lot like Dad in that she didn't have much good to say about anyone. She wasn't terribly welcome in the other houses on the hill and she didn't much like coming to ours. There was just too much that needed to be put right and Mom was never of a mind to address any of it. Gram was a pre-eminent housekeeper who had always maintained a very high standard of how everything was supposed to appear. She was very high brow, living in a world where nobody cared what she thought. Gram was a spectacular cook and she spent hours preparing the evening feast. She always made too much, ate very little, and ragged on Gramp about his weight. She put her foot down about cigars in the house but Gramp could always smoke his pipe, which she considered to be only slightly more civilized. Had to keep it in his office, though.

Grams' grandfather had fought in the Civil War and she kept a medal he had won at Gettysberg next to his picture. I think the medal was just for showing up. His name was Lord Butler Overbeck but it was never clear about whether he was royalty or just had a fancy first name. Gram's father was a rug dealer of very fine imported carpeting and her spotless custom home was more than deserving of the priceless Persian and Oriental rugs. There was a majestic grandfather clock that came from Italy that might have been made in the 1700's. It stood silently in the corner of their living room because nobody knew how to get it to work. There was a mantle clock that dispatched a deep and resonant chime and mahogany casing held all of the fancy artifacts Uncle Dickie sent home from the Phillipines when he was in the SeaBees. Gram and Gramp were pretty well off and they were very good to all of us. The best stuff at Christmas always came from them but Gramp would always just say:

"That's what grandparents are for..."

Gram hated Dad from the very beginning and he hated her right back. Gram had talked herself blue in trying to get Mom away from Dad but she married him just the same. The back story is that Dad had left Mom to serve in the U.S. Air Force in Panama where international tension was a little high and the details of his assignment are a little vague. He wasn't a spy or anything like that – it's just that there are only a couple of stories that Dad ever told. One is about how he dropped the hammer on the commanding officer of the base who sped clear through the guard post in a civilian vehicle. They wanted to court martial Dad for planting a .45 round in the guy's dashboard but the CO promoted him to corporal instead. The other affair involves a Panamanian woman who got in the way of Dad holding out for Mom.

While Dad was gone, Mom went out with another guy that everybody knew and there's opinion that he might have been her pre-connubial first. No one admits to telling Dad, but I can't imagine any less than the four or five guys it would take to keep him back. Nobody died or even got arrested but it sure had to throw the tough guy a curve about how to proceed with the woman he thought he still wanted. One of the Uncle Bob's put it right to him - either you love her or you don't; the past should be allowed to die away. And didn't Dad have a history of his own to consider? Gram - clueless as any parent then or since - kept at her about not marrying that vulgar so and so. Gram would have you know that Mom was the daughter of prominent parents who could certainly expect better in a son-in-law. Before she looked old, Mom looked good. And wasn't that nice boy from the funeral home still calling? Still, Mom only had eyes for Dad if Dad would still have her, even if it meant that Mom would pay all of her life for that one alleged original sin.

Later on when Mom got sick, it was Gram who made sure we all ate and took baths and she was quite startled to learn that we walked around naked in front of each other. We were pretty young and didn't care a whit nor did Mom but when Gram got to see this up close and personal, she wasn't having any. So any time Gram was around, we had to have some pants on and we had to wash our hands a lot. Any time that you emerged from the bathroom it was always the same:

"Did you wash your hands??

So we'd splash some water in the sink to make it sound as though we did and she would ask just the same. She never caught on because she was always old.

We got into classic rock about the same time the next door cousins got a billiard table since the two went together on a dreary winter day when there was nothing else to do. Uncle Bob picked up a regulation table that needed some work and set it up for us in their basement along with a decent radio. Everything was AM radio then because FM was only playing the old fogey stuff and hadn't gotten into stereo yet. We spent a lot of time there arguing about favorite DJ's, Ford versus Chevy versus Chrysler, and who ever needed BEATLE luvin'girls, anyway. We used to switch back and forth between WPRO and WICE for whoever wasn't playing THE BEATLES. We were good and sick of THE BEATLES but serious rock was still finding its' legs and all the other radio stations were playing crap like Lawrence Welk. Mom listened to Sherm Strickhouser who was a talk – show favorite of housewives throughout Rhode Island and Gram listened to "WEAN plus WPJB-FM in Providence" which would put you right to sleep. For me it was first and foremost THE BEACHBOYS just like Johnny Ekdahl and all the other motorheads of our time and it didn't matter that most of us had never even seen a real surfboard. The album jacket from "Surfin' USA" was enough to conjure up the California life of beaches, bikinis and hot rods. We were already building the hot rods; question was, would we live long enough to drive them – legally, that is.

Me and David saved up about six bucks and bought a brand new radio to have on the table between our beds upstairs. By 6 AM Salty Brine might proclaim "No school, Foster – Glocester" and that would be the first alert that there was enough snow to hope for a day off. Mom wouldn't just take our word for it so she listened pretty close on her own radio for a day that would have five kids in it. I never much cared for Salty Brine because he liked to listen to himself too much and he'd talk right over a good song but he announced "no school" like it was the second coming. We wouldn't budge until he was through it for the third or the sixth time and hope would fade to reality and we'd have to hurry to make the school bus. We'd see about half a dozen snow days a season back then because the rural parts of the city were truly out in the woods. Before they remade Scituate Avenue you would need tire chains to get to where we lived because it was all uphill. Even the snowplows had trouble and a true nor'easter would leave a foot or more of snow. On Charcalee Drive we were even more isolated because Gramp had this little WW II Jeep with a plow and he would clear out just enough to make the passing city trucks think we had already been done. Sometimes he would get the Jeep so mired in mud and snow that Dad had to pull him out and finish the job. This infuriated Dad because he had snow plowing of his own to do but sometimes even *he* knew when to shut up. When Caito & Chartrand paid bonuses at Christmastime, I suspect we got one also.

One time when I was in second grade, they closed school early because of a pretty good storm. It was snowing pretty hard and there was already about eight inches down and more on the way. By the time the school bus got to the bottom of old Scituate Avenue, there were only three of us left on the bus – me and Jimmy Buco and his older sister. The bus driver who was also a cop decided that he couldn't make the uphill run without tire chains so he stopped the bus and told us all to get out. We were right across the street from Quimby's gas station so the bus driver must have figured we'd have a place to call our parents from. Since it was always drilled into me not to get off anywhere but my bus stop, I wouldn't. Next thing I know, this guy plucks me out of my seat and tosses me out into the snow. Together we all trudged up a long driveway to a house where the lady knew our mothers. Dad was at work but Mr. Buco chained up and came for us, dropping me off at home. When Dad got home and Mom told him what had happened, he never even took off his coat. He jumped in his truck and went down to the police station where there were probably too many cops around to give that guy the beating he deserved. Instead, we got another bus driver who turned out to be Mike – the guy I had even more trouble with.

When they remade Scituate Avenue it was one of the biggest projects the west side of Cranston ever saw. Dad had a contract or maybe not even permission to clear cordwood from the intended route and he made a lot of money on that. They doubled the width of the road and straightened it out so much that we could race on it in a number of places. Then they posted the speed at 35 mph which everybody ignored. Butch Ekdahl got the first hundred dollar ticket and he paid it rather than lose his license. That would be more like a thousand dollars today and it was such a big deal that it made it into the newspaper. The Ekdahls built Fords - very fast Fords. I popped my very first clutch with Johnny Ekdahl and it left the driveshaft of his mother's car on the driveway on a Sunday afternoon. I was amazed that his dad didn't wig out over it like mine would have but Butch had to take us to the junkyard to get a u-joint so we could get the car back together before Monday. Butch had a 406 tri-carb in a 56' Ford and Johnny had a Mustang with a high performance 390. I was driving a slant six Barracuda fastback and the cousins started out in a Studebaker. The woods cars were all junk by now, the horses were ancient history and I lost one of my lives in the Barracuda.

The Barracuda came soon after dad brought home the 55'

Chevy that I first drove. I hated the Chevy, even though some guys were hopping them up pretty good even then. This one held zero potential because it was a four door army surplus sedan with a six cylinder and "three on the tree" shifting. It was painted a dull greenish gray - ugly as sin - and it was in immaculate condition. "Dependable transportation" Dad called it and in his mind, he had fulfilled his promise of a car if I played football. I felt otherwise and I refused to even drive it, preferring to take the school bus instead. Dad was furious; threatened to sell the car and replace it with nothing and I could just walk, for all he cared. Then he took over the Chevy and I drove one of two International Scouts' he had acquired. The Chevy disappeared, and though it was a 55', I wouldn't even want it today. It was butt ugly.

I don't know what inspired the purchase of the Barracuda unless it was a hell of a deal but it was far and away more than I had ever dared to expect. You could never tell what might strike Dad's fancy and it might have just caught his eye as he was driving past Puritan Motor's one day. It was a 1965 fastback with a 225 slant six and another "three on the tree". I could live with the shifter on the steering column because at least it wasn't a prissy automatic and I could always power shift. The car was all black with a gold interior and vinyl bucket seats. You could fold down the back seat and the back deck and stare at the stars through the massive back window. Every so often Dad would take the car to work if he was driving local, just so I couldn't say it was my car. That stopped after a half gallon bottle of milk broke on the passenger side and we could never quite get the smell out of the carpet. I drove the Barracuda all through high school and even after I quit college. It would take a 283 Impala in a walk and stay right with a 327 but I seriously overestimated our handling capacity. I had put some decent wide tires on the back but it still wasn't a Camaro and one night the back end broke away as I was screaming through a downhill turn on Scituate Avenue. The car spun like a top at least twice and even now, 40 years later, that telephone pole still flashes past. Slowed me down a bit.

Dad was a wheeler-dealer and there was always something else in the driveway. He'd buy something that needed a little work, drive it for a while, and then flip it for something else. We had a 40' Ford in the back yard that had a 394 Olds in it with a pair of four barrel carbs but it wasn't finished and it never ran. Dad said to leave it alone because it wasn't ours or his and then he sold it to one of the LoPresti brothers and we never saw it again. Cars and trucks came and went but I always had the Barracuda and it was my identity for quite a while. In high school, some of the rich kids went through cars one after another and the lot was full of hot new Mustangs, Camaros and Corvettes. Ralph Mancini had a beautiful red StingRay but he never acted like a rich kid. Debbie Martin had a pretty hot 350 Camaro. I never really saw it go, but word was that Debbie could mark a standing quarter with the best. Everybody wanted Bob Cicerone's 440 Charger, especially after the shop teacher took it down Metropolitan Avenue so fast that the car looked about 18 inches tall. Before they opened the new stretch of Route 295, we used it as a drag strip. Sometimes the cops would show up if somebody reported the noise but we'd race with them, too. I watched a Rhode Island State Police cruiser with a 426 Hemi trash a Mustang 429 Cobrajet one night and it wasn't even close. Cranston police could only sit and watch in their 318 Fury III's. Me and Lenny Colucci dragged a five dollar hole shot across from the school, right in front of Johnny Knowles' house while Johnny's dad (the cop) was standing in his driveway. Mr. Knowles sent word through Johnny that he would take my driver's license if there was ever a next time.

I couldn't have the car at URI. An incoming resident freshman did not need the distraction of waiting wheels, they said. No matter – there wasn't any parking. I lived in 112 Butterfield where they tripled us up, crowded as it was. Soon they'll triple us up in nursing homes, if there are any. At Butterfield Hall, me and Fred Schuster got really good at killing flies while Tony the Really Good

Student got to graduate. Fred majored in painting a majestic canyon creation on the wall of the great room that served as the student lounge near the entry. We almost never saw Tony since he was always at class, but across the hall from 112 there was always someone hanging out. Keith had a reel to reel of "Tommy" and it played continuously whenever Willy Wilhelm wasn't producing sharp little rifts that never seemed to go with anything. Willy lived for his guitar but he wasn't a music major and Jeff, who played a fine trumpet solo back in Tenafly, should have been. Sean taught me to love "Wooden Ships" and we almost named our son after him.

Butterfield Hall was well below the "quad", the rectangular acreage that was surrounded by stone and ivy tradition. Butterfield Hall rose above Butterfield dining room where you exchanged paper food coupons for whatever you wanted to throw at somebody else. It got so bad that they had to have campus security in attendance for a while. Later on, some others who were skilled in the art of entry raided the commissary and sponsored a miniature "Woodstock" down at Hundred Acre Pond. That caper has yet to be solved. There was weed but not a lot and I didn't really care about it at the time. All those lectures from Gram sank in and no pothead around here was going to get me, the Eagle Scout, addicted. According to Gram, all you had to do was get started and the next thing you know, you've suddenly become part of your own generation. Couldn't be having any of that, now. The frat houses were all recruiting and there were some that would make "Animal House" look tame. There'd be more than a few people passed out on the quad some nights and there was a drop-in center where you could save yourself from jumping off a roof is you could just get there. The cops got serious with the dealers and there got to be a lot of undercover and I know one kid who got five to fifteen years on an LSD charge. His wake-up call one morning was a gun barrel nudging his temple and then we never saw him again. I also know who turned him in.

Even after I was off to live at URI, Dad never sold the Barracuda. It sat in the back yard un-insured for a while so if I was home to be with Ellen, I had to take Dad's Fury III. Dad always had a truck or two to drive which worked out because nobody could take Mom's Ford wagon. When Dad the big shot truck driver crashed the last one, the new rule got passed along to include me. I only drove that car once in my life – up on 295 where we used to race. It was a '65 Ford Galaxie station wagon with a 352 four barrel that always died in the rain. Me and David stomped on it for a mile or two just to see what it could do and maybe blow out a few cob-webs and then Mom said we made it too fast

WORKIN'

I entered the world of working for sustenance right after my first date. I hadn't wanted to come up short for that first big impression I needed to make so I asked Dad for a five in addition to what I had. In TV world kids could do that whenever their parents had forgotten to first offer but in my world there was only stark reality. Dad forked over the five and silently conveyed that there wouldn't be another. He didn't go off like he could have, not even a little explosion. Maybe he was just restraining himself to make the larger point which was that he was always sitting on a pile of cash he could say no to, and don't you forget it. Nobody ever knew how much, probably because that wallet didn't come out too often.

There were farms all over western Cranston and it seemed that everybody started out picking beans. String beans, for 50 cents a bushel. But it was an income, especially for kids who lived nearby and didn't have the means to go anywhere else except on our bikes. We'd hoe tomatoes and peppers for Al Judge and Mikey Perrigino and sometimes for Mikey Pistol but at harvest we'd be in school and they had to rely on moms and anyone else who could work a fall schedule. It was hot, grimy, thirsty work and as soon as I was driving, I started looking for something better. I was a busboy, a short order cook; I filled donuts at four in the morning before school. Anything to get off of the farm and we didn't even have a farm. I worked a winter of Saturdays for Bill Stamp shoveling chickenshit out of a chicken barn window and into a dumptruck. Me and Bill and the Taylor brothers. We'd go into a hen room that you had to crouch to enter and when we were done you could stand straight up and not touch the ceiling. You'd have clear sinus for the rest of the week. We cleaned out two a day and Bill Stamp worked right along side of us, even though he and his dad owned the farm. Bill earned a college degree in how to be a farmer and he eventually built Stamp Farms into a major agribusiness. Last I heard, they had expanded into a parcel down Kingston way, got completely out of chickens and entirely into corn. Stamp Farms always had the best corn in Rhode Island and nary a bug to be found.

Filling donuts was a hoot. Joel Feinberg and his wife Rosalee owned a store in the Mr. Donut franchise. I love donuts and I just happened to ask about a job there at a time when they needed someone. I had to be in by 4:30 in the morning and I'd work for about two and a half hours before school as a "finisher". I pumped jelly donuts full of too much jelly, powdered up the sugar raised, and tried to get a head start on the mountain of pots and pans that would still be there when I came back after school. After about a month, Joel very quietly took me aside and whispered that I would be getting a raise – a whole dime an hour – but I wasn't to share this honor with anyone.

Me and Steve Stensen were the first two bus boys hired by the International House of Pancakes when it first opened in Cranston. For $1.70 an hour we used to race each other at clearing tables, breakage being the only disqualifier. The waitresses were supposed to share tips with us but that never got enforced, yet some would complain long and loud to the owner whenever they felt slighted. We really liked Terri who was about 17 when she worked there right along side of her mom. Terri had a daughter by some walk- away Joe and she pretty much had to leave her childhood behind on short notice. Terri and her mom were a good team and they were always good to the busboys and we were good to them right back. I dated the owner's sister for a while which only got me the crappy hours so that he wouldn't appear biased – and she wouldn't share, either. We reported to a scrawny little tough guy named Henry who was "third cook" and who didn't matter to us at all. Henry claimed to be an ex-Marine and he showed us how tough he was by shaving his dry face with a straight razor in the office. The hours were hard since I had never stayed awake past midnight in my life and working until 4 AM was a whole new experience. We got to see how cops and politicians and other night crawlers behaved when no one of consequence was looking and they defined the opposite of integrity. I lasted through the winter and then I went to work for myself, mostly.

Quahogs in Rhode Island are called clams everywhere else. Clams in Rhode Island are called "littlenecks" or "steamers" - that you drag through melted butter. Quahogs are used in all manner of Ocean State seafood; raw on the half-shell or chopped into chowder or "baked stuffies" and everything else anyone ever thought a quahog could be. We dig them from boats either by tong or by bullrake and you wouldn't want to get hit too hard by anyone who does this for a living. Then came the divers who could really clean out a shellfish bed. For a while there was a bit of a conflict between the divers and the rest of us but a few holes got chopped in a few boats and after the law stepped in, everybody seemed to move on. We had a quahog skiff in the water that had just enough of an outboard motor to move it along if there wasn't too much chop. I used to take it out of Warwick Cove and across Greenwich Bay to the mouth of Green River to dig in shallow water. Dad had bought a pair of 12′ tongs the year before with the greatest of intentions and he used them about twice. So I took over the boat and the tongs and I followed the tides for a summer. Sometimes Gramp would come along and sit in the bow to fish for the flounder that would gather by stirring up the bottom. In the morning I would dig quahogs and in the afternoon, I cut grass.

Dad used to take his pals fishing on my gas but since he was paying Nick the Pirate to dock there, it might have almost been fair. Once, Dad went down to the boat and the motor was missing. He had painted it a bright orange so it stood right out and when he told Nick, Nick seemed to know just who had the motor since it had just walked by his kitchen window about an hour before. Nick put a pistol in his pocket and had that motor right back.

There wasn't anything that went on up and down the waterfront that Nick didn't know about, so I always stayed on Nick's good side. That same summer, I also took a job as a detail man at a used car lot where I got to drive a '69 Jaguar XKE 2+2 coupe. It's a little scary how 80 mph can feel like 50 but my very first traffic ticket was actually for taking a right on red before you could take a right on red. Cousin Paul the lawyer got it fixed so my insurance rates wouldn't go up.

I never worked for Gramp; none of us did. We never asked, nor were we invited. You would think that a summer job in construction would be a given for us and the cousins but how would Gramp choose any of us without taking all of us? Caito & Chartrand never took on more work than they could properly manage and Gramp wasn't interested in growing the business. He didn't have to - there was always a line at the door. And Gramp was a whiz at "figuring" which was the only time we couldn't bother him. When Gramp had everything in front of him he would painstakingly calculate the cost of time and material as well as the cost of his subcontractors and he would do it with a pencil and rule right off of the blueprints. Nowadays they just aim high and double it if they don't trust the computer. Gram was his office help and she would put everything through the mechanical adding machine and type it all up on a reel to reel typewriter like the one you used to see behind Andy Rooney. But sharp as he was, Gramp agonized for weeks over the real need for adding another truck until the sons argued for the security of a locked van. That generation never got past depression era conservatism and expenses were carefully managed.

I worked for Uncle Steve the Austrian a couple of times. The first time, I was about 12 when Mom agreed to how I'd be spending one particular Saturday. Uncle Steve would be picking me up bright and early and I would spend the day painting the outside of his studio in the Alice building in downtown Providence. Uncle Steve was a portrait photographer who learned his trade in the

U.S. Navy. He was stout and he was gruff and he smoked Camel's. It was Uncle Steve who tagged my sister with "Jezebel Jazzy" although Jazzy would answer to neither. Uncle Steve was an in-law, married to Myra who was Gram's younger sister. They had married rather late in life and they had no children. The back story is that Myra (the opposite of Gram) had been married and divorced at a time when divorcee' could only mean a fallen woman. Myra had all of Gram's sophistication and none of her prejudgment or bias. Myra would take a drink as well as a smoke, leaving red lipstick on the quarter inch trademark of a Parliament.

"Your grand-ma-ma doesn't approve"

At Christmastime, Myra always wore a red beret and a Scotch plaid muffler. At the studio, they worked together and Uncle Steve would try to bark orders at her. Myra would accentuate the point of ignoring him when he got too feisty.

"Who else could work for him." She'd say.

Uncle Steve was one of those guys that you could almost never please. His diction was accented from the old world, delivered by jackhammer. He could get very angry very fast and he didn't want any backtalk whatsoever. He wasn't quite as fearsome as he was formidable - you just didn't want to take him on. And he didn't know any more about painting than I did. All he knew was that the outside of Gabermann Studios was beginning to look a little rustic and the landlord didn't care. Uncle Steve decided that we'd paint this awful shade of pink over a time worn and weary beige and it had to be done in one take. I'd be painting with a pan and roller and he'd look in on my progress every few minutes to point out where I'd missed and where I'd gotten it all over the woodwork. No one thought to mask or improvise an edger.

"You missed this whole area; do it again".

"I already did it twice – it's dry, already"

"Don't tell me; you don't know anything about this. Do what I say!"

"But that's what it looks like after it dries!!"

"And sloppy, sloppy, sloppy!! Clean that up before it sets!!"

And so it went until Uncle Steve decided that there was enough paint on the wall to hold it up. I got paid and Uncle Steve took me home – smiles all around.

I took a job at George's Restaurant and Bakery as a short order cook in the afternoon after school. It was a popular local's restaurant when George retired and Tony took it over and he was my friend, the baker from where I used to fill donuts. Tony taught me how to cook all the simple fare that had made the restaurant popular over the years but the real talent was in the baking. George's confection was legendary but Tony's was unsurpassed. I never got into any of the baking, but now I could call myself a short order cook, even though the afternoon lull was never all that busy. After I married Wife and became a commuter to URI, I went to work for a local chain called "Lums" - just across from the airport. At Lums I learned about how you can't un-cook roast beef and of the new restaurant concept of portion control. We always used to just throw a handful of something into the friolator and call it enough. Now everything had to be weighed and counted. One of the trademark logos was "hot dogs steamed in beer" which somebody invented by dumping a mis-pour into the hot-dog bath. I worked with beautiful blonde Wendy and her equally beautiful pal Maureen who was fiery and red. Chester was the manager who had to ride herd on his own senile dad until one of them got fired for touching some of the girls. Shortly after I left, the brains behind the franchise passed away and the other partners quickly ravaged the till until one by one, the stores closed up.

Hard working people are an inspiration because they lead by example. Walk the walk, never fall off of the straight and narrow - hold our society together. Immigrant labor fits the description, mostly because of what they came here to do. A number of average white guys I've known also fit the description. Dad was one; seemed he could teach himself to do almost anything he needed and he always hustled at something for a little tax free jingle. Dad understood the underground economy since American cash is the next best thing to gold and nobody's really running around with real gold. A lot of people will take less in cash if there's no paperwork involved and that worked for Dad just fine. The only time that didn't work out was when Dad knew a couple of brothers who were steeplejacks who owed him $300. One fell off the top of one of those giant industrial smokestacks and took the other one with him. Dad showed us that smokestack and told that story about twelve times and it wasn't the steeplejacks that he mourned.

Don McNally was another hard working guy that I'm glad I got to know. We were weekend short order cooks at the Arbi, named for Art and Bill who owned the place with a third partner named Haig whose name never appeared. Haig didn't want to be identified because he was once a resistance fighter with a storied past on the winning side of a WWII underground movement. His last name was a scramble of consonants ending in the Armenian Christian "ian" that I could never pronounce. The three of them held an honorable partnership and they were good enough to the help and they prospered. It was one of those little places you'd drop in on after a movie or maybe just because nobody felt like cooking at home.

Don – who was older - worked a day job for Browne&Sharpe, a Rhode Island manufacturer of world class machine tools. On weekends Don worked at the Arbi holding the kitchen together during the Saturday night blitz. He smoked PallMall's alongside my Marlboro's and he'd tell me what to make next and I'd do it. A good short order cook is a master of memory and multi-tasking - especially when the place got busy - and I had the hardest time learning that skill. I tried not to be just another task for Don, but he knew how to make the best use of what I could accomplish. I'm very good at a friolator or a broiler. Stovetop, I might be a little better now. Don could do it all and make it look easy and he never got rattled except when the girls failed to pick up. Then you'd hear that call bell all over the restaurant. Claire who was very Catholic prayed for my wife and new baby. Kaye was pals with my mother-in-law, and Evalina tried to get me to go home with her.

Childbirth had gone as planned which is to say that a room full of guys waited to hear about their new-born offspring while our women did all the work. Nobody was allowed in like they do today nor was anybody admitted to visit who wasn't an adult. Post-partem, Wife had developed a blood clot and she had to be hospitalized on blood thinners until it dissolved and it took 31 days. There would be no mother/child bonding throughout this event and Wife would get to spend a lot of time alone in her misery. Mom and Mother-in-law took turns helping with the baby so I could work and go to class and visit at the hospital. I was in summer session at the University of Rhode Island where I also had another gig helping a grad student wade through what passes for English composition in a special class for athletes. I was back and forth and upside down and when sanity began to prevail, Dad told us we had to move out of the basement, that it was all too much for Mom. Don helped me a lot because he listened and he was encouraging, almost like an older brother. I was scattered in the kitchen and Don made it work so that I could work. I have always been grateful to Don for that, so I'm saying it here in case maybe I didn't already.

My first ever full time job was with Maine Caterer's as a night cook in the commissary. I had never worked nights as in *through the night* and I learned handily about the hours I never wanted to do again. Some people like to work nights but I'm certainly not one of them – takes the living right out of life. Bill Maine was a captain on the real fire department but he owned this business on the side and David DeMatteo asked him to hire me since another guy had just quit. Bill Maine knew me and liked me enough and gave me a job when I really needed one since Dad was throwing us out. So as much as I hated nights, I sucked it up and did as I was told until driving a catering truck became available. Then I would come in at four or five in the morning and run hard until four in the afternoon. It got me off of the dreaded night shift but it also marked the end of any college future for the time being.

MPFD

Dad was a volunteer fireman any time he wasn't working or sleeping or so we thought. Growing up in Meshanticut Park, it just followed that you'd get to be a volunteer so that you could ride the truck while the old guys played cards in the back. Then your sons would grow up to be volunteer fireman so you could just sit and play cards. Gramp was a social member of long standing but he never bothered with it much except for the monthly meetings that would get him away from Gram for a while. He had once been a Civil Defense warden back in the war so he might have decided that he'd done enough.

The fire station was a great place to hang out. The engine room housed the truck and all the turnout gear that hung in order of rank. "First crew" was a special designation that rewarded you with your own assigned turnout gear, chosen from the best that was available. Second crew gear hung on a separate rack and it was always up for grabs. I always kept a selection hidden under another set so I could walk in and just grab it and it would always be there. You could earn first crew status by responding to a majority of calls and also by attending regular training classes. Then you would be appointed by the volunteer chief if a vacancy arose. Anybody who donned your first crew gear in your absence was subject to discipline but it rarely happened. When we were little and Dad was on first crew we were instructed that somebody from the telephone tree might call and simply say "fire" and hang up and then we were to summon Dad so that he could hurry off to help rescue somebody. Apparently the idea was to rendezvous at the firehouse but it never happened, never was there such a drama. The real drama came when someone wasn't at the fire station like he told his wife that he would be.

By the time I got to be a volunteer firefighter, Dad was over it. He was always away and even when he wasn't, he didn't care too much about being around - even at the fire station. A lot of his buddies had moved on and I certainly wasn't one of his buddies and I never much wanted him around either. I joined right after I turned 18 when I was still in high school and I found the firehouse to be a great place to cut a class, unless a call came in and it was at the high school. I made a lot of new friends in this grown-up world while some of my other friends joined up at the Oaklawn Volunteer Fire Department. Oaklawn was another small community just down the road that overlapped into Meshanticut and in the early times they were just villages like so many others before the city was incorporated. The Oaklawn Volunteer Fire Dept was Engine 5 and we were Engine 7. The 6's were on the other side of the city in Edgewood and Engine 8 and Engine 9 were so far out in the woods that you needed to pack a lunch to get there.

I would have lived there if I could – ever since fourth grade. Station 7 was right next door to Meshanticut Park School and there was a roof siren on the building that would go off and the next thing you know you'd hear the truck go out while most of me couldn't be on it. Everything in school would come to a halt until that siren blew itself out and I floated back down. Later on, I learned to drive the fire truck from Al DeMatteo. When I was still in my wooden high chair, we lived upstairs from the DeMatteos' on Cartier St. and they have known me my whole life. Al was the First Lieutenant and a designated driving instructor who was around a lot and he offered to teach me about the truck. I briefly thought about how it should be Dad the big shot truck driver that would teach his son how to drive the fire truck but when Al offered, I wasn't about to pass on it. Al taught me to how to split shift a 2 speed axle going up a hill which is only slightly less difficult than rocket science. Sometime after, one of the other volunteer companies got into an accident and it brought to light that we were driving trucks big enough to require a "chauffeur's license" – nowadays a CDL. And it wasn't only us. The real fire department had the same problem so they made a big production out of getting everybody certified so that no one who was suing the city could say we were unqualified. This was huge, because the biggest obstacle to a CDL had always been the lack of a big truck for a road test. A class II license created a whole new world of employment opportunities that filled a lot of holes for me over the years. I still don't have a Class III, mostly because I've never needed it. But Dad, who always had access to big trucks and semi's, had no interest in teaching any of his sons to drive the big rigs. Or maybe it was just me. He never offered and I only asked once.

The fire truck was a 1956 Ford cab-over with a 221 overhead valve V-8. Al and Jimmy Cornell fought like hell over how the little two barrel carburetor ought to be adjusted for maximum power but it never mattered; the truck was a dog and you needed every gear that the two-speed offered just to get up a short hill. The fire truck had a Federal oscillating siren with a foot switch on each side of the truck in case the driver was taking it out alone. A 500 GPM front mounted pump could feed a number of working inch and half attack lines or a couple of master streams when it made full pressure. We were always proud of that truck during hose test because you could crank it up pretty good and that pump never failed if you remembered to put it in gear. It was a really handsome fire truck, gold leaf letters and all. Whenever there was an officer in charge, he rode the seat while the rest of us rode the back step, just like our daddy's before us.

Back in the days of old, the volunteer fire departments were all that the city had and each was its' own separate entity with its' own governance. There were originally about 13 competing volunteer fire companies scattered among the many villages that made up the city. Some had great halls that were hired out for weddings, banquets, meetings, etc. We had such a hall where the upstairs was somewhat formal with polished wood flooring and a fieldstone fireplace that nobody ever lit. It had a huge wrap-around porch that ran in two directions for the kids to run back and forth on and a sweeping stairway that led to a number of French doors. On one expansive wall hung the parade banner Mom had made back in the fifties and there was an awards case full of memorabilia from when they used to compete in muster and softball. My Eagle Scout court of honor was held there as was the wedding party for me and Wife, just like so many others before us. The downstairs was much less decorated and it kept an industrial kitchen for the ham and bean suppers we put on and also for the Thanksgiving turkey raffle. Our Boy Scout meetings were held there every Thursday night and we even had a dedicated storeroom for all of our equipment.

The volunteer fire companies got a stipend from the city equal to one regular firefighter's salary to sort of keep things going and we could refuel at the city depot, but everything else was produced by fundraising. There were monthly meetings where the treasurer would howl about expenses and guys would argue about who wasn't pulling their weight around the station or about who should be promoted to drive the fire truck or about who was worthy of first crew. There were rivalries where guys took sides over rank and authority. Fire officers were elected by the general membership although they really should have been elected by the engine crew. I was never an officer and neither was Dad until much later when they couldn't get anybody to serve as president. It was on his watch that they bought a new fire truck – a Hahn - that the regulars tagged as "the queer blue maggot truck" because who ever heard of a blue fire truck? There was a lot of animosity between us and the regulars. They acted like they didn't need the volunteers and we acted like the city never needed them in the first place. Later on, too many volunteer companies decided that they didn't need to take orders from the real fire department and all of their charters were unceremoniously revoked by the mayor with the stroke of a pen. Their stipend and their dispatch were withheld, they sold their trucks, and now the Meshanticut Park Volunteer Fire Company is paved over as a playground, a hallowed institution no more.

A Christmas Wonder

'Twas just before Christmas and the snow had been falling hard since late afternoon. We had told her parents that we were just going down the road to see a movie and maybe for a bite to eat after and they had no idea of what we were really up to. For a while it looked like they wouldn't let her out but I explained that another couple was waiting for us and I had snow tires on and we'd be real careful. They relented and we were on our way. College freshmen, just home for the weekend.

Although we had dated the first part of the summer, I was certain that we were through. There had been no real intimacy - just that once when we got a little naked at the orientation for incoming freshmen. At that time, URI felt it useful to bring in the frosh, put us all in a dorm for a few days, and offer up a little dose of adulthood along with that first year orientation. It was something of a dry run at college life minus the classes. The nation was already hard into the sexual revolution and parents were scared to death of letting go. The drug and alcohol scene was real enough and no one could bear the thought that this was where their little girl was gonna get nailed her first time out. In the beginning, most guys had no idea of just what the opposite sex wanted or needed and Dads mostly didn't help. Girls were still indoctrinated to please as were their mommies before them but a few important parts always got left out. Like almost everybody else, I had impolitely groped my way through high school hoping to get lucky. It was always trial and error - some girls liked it and some didn't. Now we were on to college and this one still didn't.

I had let her go right after that first summer fling because I couldn't get to her like I wanted to. I liked her enough but I didn't love her although I might have learned to later on, given half a chance. There were some awkward moments because she and her sister had taken to hanging around the fire station, sitting on the stairs to the fire hall with Pop Camara and sister's boyfriend who at that time was the better of the Twogae. Guys coming in would tell me she was there so I could avoid her and pretty soon the girls gave up and went home - but they always came back. Today it would be referred to as stalking. All summer long this went on while I fell headlong for someone else who wanted me back just as much. Her name was Ellen and she lived way out in the woods and she was apart from a boyfriend who was a self - centered jerk. I got to show Ellen the great guy that was me - right up until I told her I was marrying somebody else. I held Ellen and I kissed her and she stood silent and wooden as I explained how I had to step up and do what was right and what was best and what was expected. It was my tragic loss, entirely.

Me and Wannabe Wife met up again at a college mixer at URI that fall and now it seems that Wannabe Wife has re-thought what was missing in our regard. Next thing you know she's ten weeks late but she isn't showing yet and now we're on our way through the driven snow to keep a date with a justice of the peace. It was crisp and cold and Christmas as we gathered up the others who would stand with us. We were all good friends who would eventually move on but on this night we would all be together as young and excited and adult as we saw ourselves. We got to Mr. McDonnell's house in good order to find that Mrs. McDonnell had decorated nicely just for us, or maybe for the holidays. Mr. McDonnell pronounced us husband and wife and after a quick stop at the Arbi for a bite we returned to our respective homes for the night and then back to URI the following Monday without telling anybody else. Then I told Dad who would handle Mom who would tell Gram who would tell everybody.

NewWife's parents were always an entity unto themselves. Hers was a household where Mom enforced the Catholicism that Wife had grown up with along with a few repressive rules of her own choosing. Her Dad would never express otherwise and their decrees were always without exception. I had found most of their values to be irrelevant and without sound reason since I had managed to seduce their daughter anyway; I didn't care too much about her Mom's disappointment. I felt sorry for her Dad, though. He was a really good Dad to all of his children and he didn't deserve to feel as though he had failed. When we finally made our way back to introduce ourselves as husband et ux et soon to be with child, they pledged to help us as much as they could. And they were greatly relieved that we would have the marriage convalidated to be officially Catholic.

The Convalidation took place later on in the winter. It is essentially a short wedding ceremony - a formality that you had to endure if you want to become an officially Catholic wedded family. It requires great preparation with serious instruction from a Catholic priest who would have no experience about how to live together as husband and wife. But true Catholics push for this hogwash anyway and there were a lot of hoops to jump through. As the college semester drew to a close, it was decided that we'd live in the basement on What a Jolly Street, at least until the baby came. But even though we were legally married, it seemed that we should get this convalidation thing over with before we appeared to be actually sleeping together. I dropped in on Father Ed who was now at St. Ann's when he wasn't the Boy Scout chaplain at Camp Yawgoog and the more I spoke, the more graven he became. Father Ed explained that there would have to be months of preparation and prayer and council and such and we were to remain mostly apart throughout. I wouldn't hear of it; untenable; non-negotiable. I would love this woman and be loved in return and there wasn't a moment to be lost. Besides, we were grownups now with a child on the way and the sex was legitimate enough to continue. Let's not close that door just now.

As it happened, URI had a chaplain who also served at Christ the King Church nearby. He was young and cool and on days he was off, so was his collar and he headed for the ski slopes. He offered us a couple of Friday afternoon sessions that would still get him to Vermont or New Hampshire in time for dinner and then he signed off on our instruction completely. The ceremony almost didn't happen because young priest handed us off to old priest on the eve of the blessing so he could take off as usual. But he had told us to go to the chapel while old priest was waiting for us at the church across the way. Old priest was actually the pastor whom we had never met but he greeted us warmly and pronounced us man and wife just the same. The in-laws were more than satisfied that there was now enough Catholic in all of this begattin' and we were kind of proud for having pulled it all together, even if it was just to please them. I could never tell you the date though, even if it is the official Catholic version of our wedding anniversary. It might even still matter somehow because in Catholic world, exWife and I could still share a bed without sin unless there is an annulment that I am unaware of. Remarkable, what they think.

Dad said that we could have the cellar for what seemed like years but it was only a semester plus the summer. It must have felt like a prison sentence for Wife who really couldn't go anywhere or do anything. Even after the baby came, I was always in class during the day and at work on weekends, all through the summer as well. The new strategy for my college future was to get the core curriculum completed as quickly as possible so that if life suddenly closed in, I would only have the electives left to do. It was a great plan until the baby came and Wife sustained a phlebitis – a blood clot in her calf. We had bought into the clinic plan at the old Providence Lying In Hospital that covered the prenatal care, the delivery and up to three days of hospitalization. It did not cover the 31 days that Wife would have to spend hospitalized on blood thinners and because we were a married couple, we were no longer included in anybody else's health care plan. It was Dad's idea for us to apply for welfare to cover the hospital bill and it was amazingly simple. The only rules whatsoever were to have no money and to be available for full time work or to be disabled. So I applied for welfare, collected one solitary check, and submitted the hospital bill that would soon go away. We never felt like we needed to be like all those other people that Dad hated; we just needed that one break. The blood clot resolved, Wife returned to the basement, and life resumed no better than before. Sometimes I would drop Wife off at her house for a change of scenery since she wouldn't learn to shift the Barracuda. We had something of a social life around other fire station families but we weren't of drinking age and we weren't about to get caught up in sharing bar tabs. So mostly there was just me and her and the baby and no real fun.

The volunteer firefighter life needed to continue as well and there were some guys who wanted my place on first crew and I wasn't going to give it up too easily. I got to be a regular engine driver and no one even held it against me when I took out one side of the garage doorjamb by turning out too soon. We had tone – alert radios by then and any alarm that called out Engine 7 went off right over our bed followed by a dispatch. David said that because of the ductwork, you could hear it loud and clear on the second floor. Sort of made me wonder what else he could hear. But I would respond to every alarm that I could, such was my dedication to a volunteer service that as it turned out, never really needed us. It got old for everybody except me because even with everything else going on, it was all I really wanted. The fire station had become my haven to which I always felt entitled. I had everything else all figured out - how I would do whatever it takes to graduate so I could get that good job Gram was always yammering about. I would take my last two years in Forestry at the University of Maine and then we could head off to some northwest wilderness paradise where I would make our living sizing up trees or fighting forest fires. The plan got as far as completing about half of my required courses when we were invited to find someplace else to live because Mom couldn't do this any more.

"...and if you let anything happen to that baby, you'll answer to me..."

And what he got was:

"Yeah"

And then it was over, between me and Dad. In a line that was even shorter than my sex talk, he was all done with me. After a lifetime of threats and intimidation and direction and promises, he felt no further obligation whatsoever. Dad had told everybody that I was going to college; the fact that I failed to remain had nothing to do with him.

We could have moved in with Wife's family just down the street from the fire station but I suppose one of the new rules would have been "no fire station". Instead we decided to strike out on our own, moving to Roberts Street in Artic which is an old term for downtown West Warwick. There was me, there was Wife - there was never an "Us". "We've Only Just Begun" hadn't been written yet but it wouldn't have mattered since we coexisted like the last two beans in the bottom of a can. Two beans and a baby in a two room efficiency apartment that easily held everything we owned. We did not love or celebrate the way you'd expect of a couple of nineteen year old kids who had just been emancipated. I had taken the night cook's job at Maine Caterer's which meant I had to sleep some time during the day. Wife would take the baby out in the stroller and window shop on Main St. for stuff we could never afford. Night shift didn't agree at all and my school work suffered so badly that I took a withdrawal from the University of Rhode Island rather than flunk out. Day in and day out, Wife had almost nothing to do except to wait for me to wake up or wait for me to come home which by now, I always did. I gave up life at the fire station and I lost my first crew status. It didn't matter much; I was too exhausted to continue as a part time fireman. Our life together was good enough in that we never went without the essentials and the baby thrived, but living so far away from all that we knew was beyond inconvenient. It was downright depressing.

Randall Street

Life changed dramatically right after we moved back to Cranston. Gramp's good friend Jimmy Canto had an empty walk-up that he had just cleaned up and we were invited to look at it. The rent was a hundred and twenty five a month heat included; Jimmy lived right next door and his addled mother lived just below us. We would be right across the street from Randall's pond where we had always fished and skated and played hockey with Johnny Bruno and a bunch of other roughnecks. It was perfect and it was ours if we wanted it and we were ecstatic. We bought a brand new refrigerator at the Ann&Hope department store that the delivery guys refused to take up the spiral stairs so me and David did it with only minor damage. The in-laws gave us a gas stove that they weren't using and now they were just up the road from us. We saw them a lot since they had fallen right in love with the baby. They were only a couple of blocks from the fire station, and they had a built-in swimming pool so it was a great place to hang. Wife had a brother and two sisters and we were all within a few years of each other. One sister had a hot and heavy romance with the best of the Twogae (whom the in-laws hated) and Wife once had something with another Twogae that she would eventually need to continue.

The Twogae were a good Catholic family of a good Catholic number including twins whom I knew variously over the years. One was my very good friend while the other was good enough to leave Wife alone. One of the Twogae had heroically pulled his brother from the nearby Pocasset River when they were about eight years old; it was all over the news. Another brother was a war hero who eventually succumbed to Agent Orange disease – got himself sent home from Vietnam with three Purple Hearts. The worst of the bunch followed his dad's example. The old man was something of a drunk and a bit of a philanderer and seldom held a steady job. They say he was a pretty good carpenter and handy man and a bouncer around the rental properties that the missus strictly maintained. The Twogae rented rooms to single men with a shared kitchen which Wife's dad had made use of when he came here alone from Chicago. He had come for a new job with better opportunities at American Hoechst Chemical Corporation, the largest single employer in Coventry, Rhode Island. Mother-in-law mourned the loss of her family and friends in Chicago but dutifully followed her husband and made herself a new life. Eldest daughter was beyond devastated to have to give up her home and her friends and her senior year at Thornridge and she never got over it until I offered her the opportunity to go back there for good. Then it suddenly didn't matter.

While we were still in West Warwick, I was invited to apply at "HershChemical" as everybody called it because father in law got to be well established as an assistant building superintendent. I was hired immediately as a helper but I had never worked in anything that even resembled a factory so this was a whole new experience with all new people and I was nineteen. I was by far the youngest in Remazol where we made the presscake that would be dried and ground into the dye that put the blue in blue jeans. There was Roger who later died of AIDS and there was SpeedyG who could have been Eddie Murphy and he was my first regular association with a black person. Armand was the batchmaker who used to be a chef and Roland was the little guy with the big attitude who would tell you straight up:

"If you don't want to work, go home."

But he never had to say it to me. Privately, while we teamed up at dropping product out of a press he would say:

"Don't get too eager – you'll spoil them. Two presses,
that's a night's work. Don't slack off since you're on probation
but don't go over or they'll always want it."

He was absolutely right because there were white hats who thought that they had to make their reputations based on how much they could get a guy to do. Then as soon as they could get it out of one guy, they'd go at everybody. This was where I got to be a big shot Teamster just like Dad because Local 64 represented labor at Hoechst. We even got to go on strike.

This was real money. Dad made more because he was with the truck driving Teamsters Local 251 but nobody around made the kind of money I was making without a college education or a bona fide trade. I was hired for second shift – three-thirty to midnight – and it worked out so well that Wife could take a morning job as a teller at the Industrial National Bank. As the baby got older he wanted to do more on his own and he required complete and constant attention unless he was fast asleep. Mom once bought him a play set of rubber pots and pans for the sand box and he tried to cook just like Mommy one morning before anybody was awake. Smoke detectors for the home weren't all the rage yet and we were pretty lucky that we smelled the fire. I put it out with a glass of water and a dishtowel but now that he had learned to climb out of his crib, we learned to listen for it. He always wanted to help, to be just like his Daddy. There were a couple of old dead apple trees that Jimmy said I could cut down and sell for firewood and I have video of KJ on the other end of a two-man saw at the age of about two and a half. We tore down an old chicken coop that Jimmy hauled away and nobody got hurt doing that, either.

We made friends across the street with Lorraine and her two kids and some of her friends who came to play MaJong during the week. Plant Street was right across from us and it went down to Randall's pond where we'd fish from shore until I got us a little rowboat to go out in. That made us pretty popular except with the neighborhood moms so I always pulled the boat back across the street and up the driveway so nobody could take it out and drown. That satisfied the moms and soon enough I was the nice guy with the adorable little boy who was also a fireman that would take their kids fishing. We also got a bicycle and a seat to mount on the front so that the child could be the first to enjoy impact. No helmets, no precautions, never had a mishap. We peddled through Saint Ann's Cemetery where we'd watch the funeral processions meander through to the receiving chapel. After the mourners had left, we'd watch as the casket was wheeled through to where they'd encase it in two halves of a cement liner, put it on the back of a truck and take it to drop in a hole with a hydraulic arm. It was purely a mechanical process unless the funeral service was graveside. "Drop another one" we called it, as in:

"Dad, Can we go watch them drop another one?"

Mother- in- law was not amused but we thought it was terrific.

I had charge of my son every morning of every weekday while Wife worked at the bank and then she'd come home in time for me to go to work except for once when I had to go yell at her boss. Bank tellers need to "settle" at the end of their day and nobody cares how long it takes. There was a vacant house lot right next door that Jimmy also owned but it was overgrown with tall weed. Years before, his mom would grow and preserve a whole year's worth of produce for the family and there was some of it stored in the cellar, probably still edible. Jimmy said I could cultivate that plot if I didn't mind clearing it and if I didn't mind his addled mom supervising. I had this great idea of growing enough tomatoes to sell and when I started turning it over, I found the soil to be a rich dark loam about three feet deep. Dad was back into farming by then and he had a space at the farmer's market where area grocers and vegetable stand owners picked out their produce for the day. I put those tomato plants in two weeks earlier than anybody would ever dare despite all of the advice I got to the contrary and pushed them with hand feedings every other day. I figured that the worst that could happen was that I'd be planting them all over again if we got a frost. It never happened and I had early tomatoes – highly prized in Rhode Island - a good three weeks ahead of anybody. I was producing better than ten handle – baskets every day on plants that grew up to my waist. Dad took the tomatoes to market along with the greenhouse flowers Mom grew and he told everybody they were his because there was something of a competition to be first with tomatoes. By the time tomatoes got down to three dollars a basket, I was taking them around the neighborhood for free and Mrs. DiBiase across the street made us a pizza that was so big we had to call reinforcements to eat it all. I made enough at that venture to buy Wife a 78 point diamond that had gotten caught up in the Nixon era price freeze, or so they said. But it was a beauty and now maybe Wife could be a little happier about being together.

Or not. Right around this time there was a bit of an issue concerning birth control in general and abstention in particular. When Wife had the blood clot, the experts agreed that she was most assuredly at risk for another and should never entertain the risk of another pregnancy. Nor should she undergo the new-fangled tubal ligation procedure that was suddenly so popular. Same risk. So I decided that our safest option would be that I should get a vasectomy because it was simple enough and would end our concerns forever. Besides, studies had shown that some women could not enjoy intimacy because of that nagging fear of pregnancy. Maybe I was married to one of those. So I went to the same clinic that had given us our son and at first blush, the doctor wouldn't do it because I was 20. We argued and I won and I became sterile forever. Our love life picked up when I would help myself to wife and she would let me and a couple of times, she even helped a little.

Jimmy had it a whole lot worse than I did. He was almost as old as Gramp and he had a serious heart condition but he was still working hard, rolling beer barrels around for a union distributor. He worked until he couldn't do it any more because he never *wanted* to be home, except to sleep. He and his wife hated the sight of each other and lived in separate parts of the house. They would leave notes for each other whenever there was an utter need to communicate and they had two teenagers learning from this. Jimmy's addled mother lived all by herself and she got to be a friend of sorts when she was lucid. She had yelled at us about something early on but I was really nice to her about it because she was so obviously addled and she liked me. She used to sit in the window and watch us bring the garden back to life. But she was older than old and I'd look in on her almost daily and sometimes I'd find her sitting with a military photo of her dead son along with a collection of some of the official Catholic saints, wailing away. Towards the end of our stay there, the old lady took to rapping her cane on the stairwell for attention and we figured it was time to move. Jimmy said that she was getting to be too unmanageable and that she would call him on the phone in the middle of the night to say that we were roller skating back and forth upstairs. Jimmy encouraged us to start looking for a house – no hurry - especially since interest rates were headed up and inflation was back to driving the economy.

Hoechst Chemical

Speedy G. Horton. He would slip in and out of character so easily that you had to be paying attention to just who was doing the talking. He was Eddy Murphy before there ever *was* Eddy Murphy. He probably wouldn't agree that Speedy G and Emmett Horton were two different people because to Emmett there was no real transition. Sometimes Speedy G would go off long and loud and maybe pontificate a little but it was pure soliloquy. He'd have everybody listening and then he'd narrow his eyes and furrow his brow and then Emmett would take over. He'd scan the room and we'd be staring at him.

"What?!!"

Emmett was my friend and he was the first black guy I was ever up close to except for Dad's friend, Billy White. But I didn't really get to know Billy White until much later and I was working with Emmett every day. There were a few black people on campus at URI but none in any of my classes and none in my dorm. There had been the riots and the protests but not here or anywhere near here so I was pretty sheltered and mostly ignorant about what held meaning for a black person. I just figured that personal dignity was something we all had in common. I had apologized for another guy who had opened a conversation with: "...what a funny nigger..." and I didn't know if Emmett caught it or not but it threw me a little so I apologized to him, anyway. To hear that word out loud carries the same snap as all the other bad words that would get your mouth washed out with soap. I was always amazed that so many black people put up with such a casual disregard for common decency. Billy White had shown such tolerance for Dad's ignorance – even called Dad a friend. How many white guys would have been so gracefully denigrated? So I felt a little responsible and a little saddened that the conversation even had to happen and Emmett just blew it off for me. He didn't know how I was raised.

So we'd pick up on whatever Emmett was on about and argue it and kick it around until after supper in the break room. We all brought lunch from home because family men couldn't afford to eat from the catering truck that pulled up by the smoke shack. Nor could we afford the card games on break where some of these guys lost way more than they'd ever admit to. But we all smoked and it was strictly forbidden anywhere on the grounds so we'd hightail it out for a quick one. Armand never smoked so he'd have his supper inside and keep an eye on the kettles and vats while we were gone. He got to be really old; he was sixty eight when he finally retired and he lived well into his eighties. He kept a little gray skiff in the back of his old Ford pickup and he spent his mornings in Nausaucket Cove fishing for what he called "buttybutts" – the winter flounder that were mostly too small to keep. After work I'd join him and Roland for a 15 cent beer at the Washington Street Café, and then I'd go right home. Sometimes I would chauffer Roland so his wife could keep their car for the night. It was a little out of my way since I had to go over the hill that was Wakefield St. from Cranston to West Warwick but it was a pretty ride and I didn't mind it. Besides, the Barracuda now had an 8 track tape player and I could listen to either Creedence or New Colony Six. Roland and Madeline had a son about my age who worked in Father in Law's building on day shift but they also had a daughter whom I thought was adorable. She was about 14 with long dark hair and coal black eyes and she was always happy. My 20 year old self still wonders what ever happened to her.

Armand was the lead batchmaker and also the acting foreman until Neville got back from Vietnam. Neville was the regular second shift foreman but his National Guard unit got called up before I was hired and he wasn't due back anytime soon. Since we didn't have Neville, nothing mattered as long as the work got done. No one took serious advantage; maybe an extra smoke or a longer break was all. We never gave Armand any crap because he was union like us except he was getting paid to be the foreman by virtue of his seniority. Union rules. But he knew the batch and he knew the building and when Neville got back, even he listened to Armand. We were a pretty good crew and we produced enough to make Neville look good but that wasn't so hard to do because the first shift only got half as much done with twice as much help and more bosses. At least that's how we saw it. Neville knew enough not to push because he saw first hand what the third shift boss failed to learn. Besides, Neville was a pretty good guy.

I liked working in Remazol because everything was water soluble, not like Pigments next door where everything was yellow. That stuff only came off with sodium hypochlorite and you had to really scrub. Somebody said that another department found out the hard way that some guys pissed in the shower. The ammonia in urine would mix with the chlorine in the hypochlorite to produce ammonium chloride fumes that could kill us all. We shared a shower with the Pigment guys but I guess everybody was toilet trained because nothing like that ever happened. Father- in- law worked in the Dioxa building and he always leached out a maroon color with perspiration and he didn't even handle the stuff. Some of the guys in Dioxa had these open sores that they took care to hide so that they wouldn't have to leave the building - too much overtime at stake. Father in law's best foreman apparently got a little too much exposure because suddenly he had cancer and just as suddenly, he was dead. This happened to a number of others over the years but it was a time when the affects of smoking were just beginning to come to light and no one gave the working environment a second thought. I always figured it was just common sense that exposure to industrial chemicals was something to take every precaution against, except for the idiots who took no precautions at all. Rubber gloves, rubber boots, respirators - basic equipment that the company was generous about providing often went unused. Later on, as they learned more about what was killing the idiots, isolation suits and bottled air and a lot more rules became the norm.

I sold the Barracuda to a guy at Hoechst who didn't love it like I did and I was happy enough when he quit so I'd never have to see the car again. Wife still wouldn't learn the shifter - adamantly refused – and would never get off of wanting something she could drive. We bought a 70' Fury III with a 383 four barrel and it was a four door hard-top with electric windows. Nice car – even Dad was impressed. We drove it to Chicago for a wedding in about 18 hours and it held 90 – 95mph without even breathing hard. It was my first loan ever and Dad had to cosign because I asked him in front of Mom. It was odd to hear him have to say out loud how much money he made - $12,500 to my $10,500 but then, that was just the paycheck money that he reported to the bank and the IRS. He always had something else going, more cash than anybody ever knew.

Dad had bought an abandoned farm that still held a lot of promise. There were a couple of old greenhouses and one was worth fixing up and I took a couple of stitches in my ass putting in new panes of glass on the roof when I fell through. Dad hadn't asked me to help but he didn't need to - I just showed up so that Dad's dream would finally make him happy enough to have us all as a real family. There were a lot of us who helped Dad out every weekend to put the farm back in shape and pretty soon there was produce growing. Dad learned to be civil enough to everyone who was working for free and Gramp supervised construction of the new house. Mom would have to get used to not being just up the street from Gram or else she could just go live with her, Dad said. But Mom chose subservience over loneliness, or maybe she didn't choose at all. Wife wanted no part of anything to do with farm life and wouldn't even go there to visit without an argument.

Never mind that Dad had sold off the tomatoes for me that bought the new rock on her hand, Wife was adamant that I would get so screwed in the end. She was wrong; it would be several screwings before there would be an end and in the meantime, Dad wouldn't care if I showed up at all.

In 72' I suffered a motorcycle crash that could have squashed me like a bug. I had a Honda CB 175 which was second generation to the old 160 that's now worth a fortune. I bought it from David so he could buy his 350; my first and last motorcycle. It made sense, what with the price of gas creeping up that I'd run the Honda to work and Wife could have the car. Pulling out onto Atwood Avenue, a lady in a big Impala stopped and waved me out as she was about to pull into the bank parking lot. Just as I crossed her path to go left, a new Dodge Challenger pulled out from behind her and ran right over the front of the bike, twisting up my front fork and mangling my left little finger. The finger never required surgery, just a re-set and some stitches. Adding insult to injury, I also got charged with the accident. This put me out of work for the entire summer where I spent mornings hoeing tomatoes and peppers for Dad and afternoons at the Curran Reservoir where I'd take everybody swimming. Two weeks out, I had to get another X-ray and Dr. William was somewhat less than pleased:

"What have you been doing?"

"Nothing."
(long, intense stare)

"Umm, hoeing tomatoes for my old man and
I take the kids swimming. That's all, honest"

So he took hold of my finger, steel splint and all, and started to pull - a little too hard. And I pulled back but he's a big guy and now he had my whole arm over the top of his desk but before I knew what to do next, he came up with a medical text and slamed it down on my hand.

"No more hoeing tomatoes, Y'hear?"

Then he re-aligns the new fracture and I'm out for another twelve weeks, collecting disability insurance. And all the while, Hoechst held my job. Union rules.

So it gets to be harvest time and I'm back to where I can use the finger a little without the splint but mostly I'm just driving the flatbed through the field. Jazzy shows up to help but we start arguing about something nasty that she says about Wife and it gets ugly. I didn't think much of it because Dad wouldn't care – he never did. When the harvest money started coming in and I thought I'd at least see enough to help my own situation a little, I got my next surprise. Slouched in his fake leather chair, he pulled out his wallet and offered me a $100 bill.

"What's this?"
"Your pay"
"For the whole summer?"
"The twins got ten speed bikes; same difference."
"For the whole summer? The twins are 10;
I've got a family too, you know."
"Can't get along with your sister."

I just stand there dumbfounded. Then KJ crawls up on Dad's lap and Dad just coldly picks him up and plops him on the floor. Stupefied no longer, our first real estrangement begins.

I got back to Hoechst in September to find that they wanted to break in another batch maker on second shift because Armand was about to retire. I bid for it and I get it because nobody else wants it and by now Neville's back to being the foreman. I had never met him before this but he seemed O.K. enough and besides,

Armand would be teaching us both. By now Armand was saying some of the same things over and over to where it would get your attention but we always thought he was just getting old, like Jimmy Canto's addled mom. But he knew every detail of every process and he was the only one that could get the cranky old acid scrubber to work without fumigating the building. Management was pretty happy to have me in this position because I could follow directions and I already knew the vats, the kettles, and the lines that supplied material and delivered product. The Pawtuxet River ran right behind the plant and dyestuff's in the river would bring a severe consequence. We had a guy on the day shift that would intentionally overload an acid charge with bicarbonate of soda and the product would rise up out of the vat and crawl down the walkway like a scene from "The Blob". It would have been hilarious if it weren't so serious because it would clear the building for hours and the bosses had to don air packs and clean it up.

I liked being a batchmaker well enough and I never suffered a serious mishap. If a batch couldn't be left to itself through supper, I'd have my sandwich right there and then Neville would watch it for me against union rules so I could run out for a smoke. By agreement, the company was supposed to pay time and a half if you were directed to work through your break but I cared more about a cigarette than I did about the money. When Neville was out for a surgery, they made me the working foreman of the second shift, just like Armand had been. I was 21 and had never been the boss of anybody but the shift ran itself, just like it had for Armand. Another 50 cents an hour for nothing! Then Remazol got really slow and they closed down our shift and farmed us out all over the plant. I worked in Pigments for a while which was right next door but when Pigments got slow I ended up in "Poopsie's" building in the finishing department where I had my first and only individual confrontation with management.

Poopsie got his name because that's what his wife called him and somebody heard it. Sorry for his trouble, but if your wife is dumb enough to let that out in front of a bunch of union roughnecks, you own it. Poopsie was the director of the finishing department which had a number of machines and processes that had nothing to do with anything I had ever done in Remazol. Norman the Foreman was an idiot who had no idea of how the place worked either so he couldn't offer any instruction and he would put me to work at one project, only to pull me away to start in on something else. He never knew how to manage priorities or personnel and he never stuck around to supervise, preferring instead the comfort of the air conditioned office. It all came to a head when second shift production came to a grinding halt over an intermediate they needed that had not yet been finished. Norman passed the blame on to me, even though I had been assigned to another operator as a helper. He tried to concoct a grand story of how uncooperative I was and that he couldn't get me to fulfill the simplest task. I was amazed that this wasn't handled in-house but Poopsie didn't know who to believe so he punted the whole affair to personnel – HR by today's definition. Father- in- Law was called to attend, mostly so that he could witness for himself of how fairly I would be handled but I was a bit shocked by his presence. At the hearing, I had requested union representation and a written indictment was read and Norman tried to add to it. I was able to refute each and every charge and I even made a few of my own. I asked that they simply ask anybody over at Remazol about my work ethic, not realizing that of course, they already had. On the way out, I apologized to Father in Law about having brought him into the mix but he brushed it off. He told me that I could stand for myself just fine – that none of this would be seen as any of his responsibility. Turns out, it was all a charade. They were just looking for enough documentation so that they could fire Norman, which they eventually did.

Wife and I had been saving money all along when the Intermediates building got really busy and there was a lot of mandatory overtime. I got to bid over there because nobody else wanted it and I started working double shifts so that we would be able to buy a house. Wife was still at the bank and the savings account grew and we even opened a college fund for our son. Inflation would slow some because of the first energy crisis but interest rates also had just started climbing. As gasoline started to become an issue, we got ahead of the curve a little by trading the Plymouth for a brand new 72′ Datsun B-110 sedan which was the forerunner of the famous B-210. It had a 1200 cc engine and twelve inch tires that couldn't climb a curb. I had also bought a 67′ International pick-up and it was the most useful vehicle I had owned up to that time. It had a nine foot bed, 16″ tires, and a 345 V-8 that couldn't get past a gas station. The driver's side door didn't always shut tightly so every once in a while there was a little surprise if you leaned on it but that didn't stop people from wanting to borrow it. It's amazing how many people need to move stuff when you have a truck.

The estrangement with Dad ended quietly after a lot of pressure on me from Gram and Gramp. They weren't happy at all that Mom suffered because of Dad since Mom wasn't the cause of any of this except that she always backed him. So we started going to see Mom again and pretty soon we ran into Dad and nothing was discussed and nobody ever apologized. Jazzy had joined the U.S. Army which was a great relief to all except for one of the next door aunts who said it was a damn shame, that she would have scrubbed floors and cleaned toilets before any daughter of hers would join the army. But it was no secret how that aunt despised Dad. They'd had words over the years and she'd tell you straight out that Dad was a goddam liar – lie right at you and know he was doing it and she was right. I always loved her for that and for the faith she had in me because she had made a point of offering encouragement when everyone else offered criticism. And she helped Mom through a lot.

Piedmont Street

We decided that we had enough money to start looking at houses and the race was on to find one before we got priced out of the market. The interest rates that had been stable for years were now on the march in the wrong direction. We had to keep re-calculating what we thought we could afford as rates seemed to go up a quarter of a point every week. In those days, the bank wouldn't give you a mortgage if the monthly payment exceeded 25% of your monthly gross and they wouldn't include Wife's income lest she become suddenly disabled with child. There were a number of other qualifying rules as the banks looked for ways to insure themselves against default. They also wouldn't count the income from a duplex or a tenement unless you were willing to put money in escrow against a bad tenant or a vacancy. We had looked at everything that there was in the 20K range and it seemed that interest rates were now climbing daily. Our parents had always enjoyed four or four and a half per cent at most but that was when banks kept their loans and you might be sitting in church next to your local banker. We put money down on a house at 7 ½ % and by the time we locked in it was 8 ¾ and climbing still.

We looked at houses deep in the woods and we looked at a house that was about to fall down a hill. We looked at perfectly good houses that Wife just didn't like and we looked at the house that the Stickney's had died in that had to be fumigated half a dozen times. Then we found a neat little Dutch Colonial on Piedmont Street and I asked Dad to come with us for a second look. He said no so I asked Gramp who had just retired from being a home builder and he pronounced the dwelling to be fit and sound. It was listed for $19,900 and we offered $19,000 which

Mrs. Silva was happy to accept and she even left us the electric stove for $50. We had saved all but $500 of the 20% down on a conventional mortgage so I asked Dad for it. I had been working the doubles for a while and I knew I could pay him right back. It would have saved us more in closing costs and it would have saved us a half a per cent over the life of the 30 year mortgage. Dad said no, and we didn't ask anybody else.

We drove to the Old Stone Bank on Park Avenue with my pickup truck full of hope and household goods because the bank was on the way to our new home. Neither of us could afford to burn time off at work but there wasn't a whole lot to move, either. At the bank, we had no idea of what to expect except that right up until the house officially changed hands, the deal could go south. We sat among all of the official people and signed what they told us to sign and it all took so long that we thought they might even serve lunch. There was an anxious moment when somebody couldn't find a document relative to assuring the bank that it wouldn't get screwed but they produced it before I needed another breath. When it was over, we spent the remainder of the day moving in everything but the large appliances which would have to wait until Saturday so that David and I could lug that refrigerator back down the stairs. It was April, it was cold, and three days later we were out of heating oil. We filled the tank, turned up the thermostat, and burned through 500 gallons of oil inside of 30 days. The house wasn't insulated and it was heated by an ancient cast iron boiler that fed equally old cast iron radiators. There was an early version of a tankless hot water heater attached, and as it turned out, this grossly inefficient system had to crank itself up on demand just to keep a smidge of water hot. We had gotten into the house with about twelve dollars to spare and we were beyond broke. We limped along from paycheck to paycheck until the austerity paid off and summer was upon us. But anybody thinking that these hard times brought us closer together as a couple would be wrong. We just switched from oil to natural gas, put in a hot water heater, and moved on.

We were now all the way across town in a neighborhood I only knew about because it was right near Roger Williams' Park. We were well enough greeted by all of our neighbors and soon my son had a number of new friends and none of them were relatives. There was still a lot of overtime at Hoechst so we saved up our money and bought some brand new Herculon furniture, some dark pine coffee tables and matching Liberty Bell lamps. Upstairs, we stuffed a cannonball bed and a triple and a double dresser – into a 9′ X11′ master bedroom. KJ already had a brand new bed that we had bought when he outgrew his crib and now it took up most of his new bedroom. In a third bedroom we kept in storage all the stuff we had worked too hard for and wouldn't part with. I overhauled anything Wife wanted that we could afford to do and I built a rustic tool shed out of rough – edged pine just like Gramp would have. We put up frilly curtains and pronounced ourselves Early American.

Apparently our hard work and good fortune was enough to keep us right with the in-laws because they were entirely gracious and good to us and never seemed to hold much against me. We must have appeared pretty solid as a couple since everything appeared to go along so swimmingly. The in-laws got us a new washer and dryer as a housewarming present and they came to visit once in a while even though it was all the way across town. Sometimes we'd even go someplace fancy for dinner and have a real drink with them, we were so grown up. I had also invited Mom and Dad time and again because I was so proud of our new place but they only came once for KJ's birthday and Dad held court like the big shot that he thought he was. Mother in law asked later about what he was so proud of since he didn't seem to have any more than anybody else and if he did, then why was he so stingy? It was right after that when Dad cornered me and said to stop inviting them since he had so much else to do besides sit with polite company. After a while, Mom remarked that the in-laws seemed to be over all the time. When I told her what Dad had said, I could feel how much it hurt her but it hurt me too and Mom needed to know that this wasn't about any choices I had made. Dad could answer for himself if he chose to or he could continue to opt out as he had on just about everything else. Mom never required anything of Dad – not even fidelity.

Shortly thereafter, David had a falling out with Dad and needed a place to stay in a hurry. We put a price on a bedroom and established a few ground rules and another estrangement with Dad began. I had always felt bad for how David was trapped in ways he hadn't even realized. Me and Jazzy had always presumed David to be the favored one but that was mostly because he escaped the scrutiny that Dad and Mom held out for me and Jazzy. That favoritism came with a price as it seemed to fall to David to hold the farm together. Even though David had a whole other full time job, he was still captive to Dad's expectations so long as he lived there. It couldn't have been easy and one time, he fell asleep at the wheel of the Cub cultivating tractor and drove it right into the side of the greenhouse. On the very same tractor, David escaped disaster while re-connecting the battery. He had dropped a wrench and when he bent down to pick it up, the battery exploded for no apparent reason. Pure happenstance; pure luck. David would have been blinded and disfigured for life. David only stayed with us for a few weeks because Dad couldn't run the farm or get any of the other work done without him. They struck a truce but Dad also made it clear that only David was welcome back into the fold. At Christmastime, Mom sent over a pile of gifts for KJ and we sent them right back. Cold war once again became the way of our family.

Louie Fontaine and I were great friends going all the way back to St Ann's School in first grade and we made our First Communion together. He grew up to be a big bear of a guy with a bushy beard that made him look like Paul Bunyan or Pierre of the North. We were at URI together and I used to bum a ride back and forth on weekends so I could be with Ellen before second round with wannabeWife. Louie and his dad shared a commute because the nursery farm was only a couple of miles from URI where his dad was a foreman of the field crew. It was a family owned business on Louie's mother's side and there might have been a little tension about that because I never saw this guy in a good mood on his way to work. He scowled about everything and he had a special ache in his craw for his eldest son and sometimes it could be an awfully quiet ride back to Cranston. Louie's dad wasn't at all like mine but he could be just as hard to be around. Sometimes me and Louie would just sit in his car and have a beer about why our younger brothers were so favored. But Louie's dad eventually got over himself and turned into a decent guy. Or else we all just got older.

On Sundays I used to take my Early American self hunting with Louie and his dad at the nursery farm he supervised in South County. They had beagles that ran rabbits and they could go for hours on one scent if they had to. The strategy was to surround the brush or the woodland that the dogs were working and wait for a rabbit to be driven into the clear so that we wouldn't shoot the dogs or each other. Louie and his Dad had some nice shotguns and I used to use Louie's 12 gauge pump action before I was able to buy my own gun. All I could afford was a single shot Savage 12 gauge but I really wanted a 16 gauge over and under. An Ithaca if you please, or a Fox with a gold trigger. Louie's dad used to get a little steamed that I was only carrying the one round since the dogs worked so hard but I never needed a second round, ever. Never needed the first one either because in all the times I hunted that farm, we might have killed three rabbits and I never raised a gun. We were after birds, too - pheasant, quail, woodcock, grouse - but we never saw many at the nursery. There was a rental house on the property where the people had this big red dog that used to get loose and when he wasn't digging the place up, he was driving off the birds way ahead of us.

One day Louie dropped by to see if I wanted a dog that somebody needed to get rid of. He couldn't take it because he had the beagles and he thought it was time I had a dog, anyway. It made me think of Laddie and up to then, I had never really wanted to think about how much I missed my dog or even worse, the times when Laddie must have really missed me, right up until Dad shot him. So I took a ride with Louie who didn't divulge where we were going, right up until we pulled into the nursery. He said that he had to check on something for his dad and maybe I'd like to buy a bridge since all along it had been about the big red dog that was tied up short to a tree. The dog that digs foxholes; the dog that puts the birds up away from us; the dog that they needed to get rid of or else get kicked out of their house. I wanted him immediately, this big red goofy Golden Retriever but the people weren't home so we couldn't just take him. It killed me to leave him tied to that tree but it would buy me enough time to try to talk it into Wife who of course, said no. But I said yes and me and KJ went to get him and Rusty licked us silly all the way home.

I probably always knew that I was headed for the real fire department. My football career never really panned out nor had my college future. I could never fulfill the academic prerequisites to be a fighter pilot and I never even tried to enlist a NASCAR sponsor. I hadn't been on a horse in years and who ever heard of a cowboy from Rhode Island, anyway. But I knew I could be a champion firefighter and given the opportunity, I would step right up to do some pretty courageous deeds. I got in as one of our class of sixteen that would be hired so that the city could open the new Station 4 in Garden City.

First response would include the entire site of the state institutions – a vast complex of Rhode Island's incarcerated population. At that time, most of the state institutions would resemble the nuthouse from "One Flew Over the Cuckoo's Nest" but the Boys Training School was one of the newer buildings and it housed some of the worst kids anybody's god ever made. Somehow they got control and managed to bottle the place up from the inside and then they set fire to it. There were a number of deaths and one kid was even found face down in a toilet bowl. The news coverage was extensive and it very much inferred that the city was negligent since they had taken so long to open the new fire station. In return, the mayor pointed out that the state didn't contribute one dime for the breadth of protection that it was already getting.

Right after the tragedy at the Boys Training School, our new class of firefighters was suddenly called up. When I gave notice to Hoechst Chemical I was immediately summoned to the personnel department. The assistant director who had originally hired me - the same guy who knew I'd had to leave school - offered me a white hat position and tuition assistance if I would return to class and then there would be a professional opportunity once I earned my college degree. They would help any way that they could, he said. While he was speaking I thought of way back when I had been hired along with one other guy who got the job of sitting in front of an instrument panel all night. He was a high school drop-out who used to complain about how there weren't enough paperbacks in the world that could help to pass the long, boring hours. I could have easily completed my degree if they had put him to labor and given me that job instead and I couldn't imagine why they were so concerned about keeping me now, years later. So I said no.

I had finished in the top few of about 800 people who took the written test and we were placed on a hiring list that would stand for two years or until the list was exhausted. The city also decided to put the new hires through a trial on very short notice where we took the first agility test that the fire department had ever required. The test was created by people who couldn't quite remember how it was done in their army days so they guessed at it. Pushups, situps, and two laps around Fay Field on a 90 degree day in fire boots qualified all of us who would be the first line of defense in any conflagration. But they kept putting off the actual appointments until some got too close to the age limit and all of us were worrying that the hiring list would expire. Of greater concern was a rumor we were hearing about connected people getting to jump the line, so I went to see Gramp.

Gramp was a brother in law to U.S. Senator John O. Pastore who also used to be the governor. He was known about as the "do – nothing" senator, a gifted orator who was always tooting the party's horn. But he was squeaky clean and he was close to the Kennedys from the very beginning so as a loyal and valuable Democrat in a Democratic state, he was in for as long as he wanted it. John O. Pastore was the keynote speaker at the 1960 Democratic convention that nominated JFK and he was a good distant relative to have if you knew just how to drop his name. He lived in Cranston and his address and phone number was in the phone book and you could actually just call him up. Which I didn't; I asked Gramp first. As it happened, we never needed the senator. Right before my very eyes Gramp called up his old friend Tom Powers who was the chief of the Cranston Fire Department. Turns out, they both belonged to the Kiwanis International – a popular club for gentlemen who would be of service to the community. "Serving the Children of the World" is their stock in trade although from one locale to the next, they do much more. After a few words that I wasn't privy to, Gramp hung up and told me to go see Chief Powers the next day, no appointment was necessary. I was elated; everybody who ever knew Tom Powers would tell you that he was the first guy ever that really knew how to be the chief of this department. He never sweated the small stuff, he never turned against his men, and no one ever thought that he wasn't in charge. If he wanted me, I was in. I don't know how nervous I might have appeared when I went to see Chief Powers, but for the life of me I couldn't figure out the latch to the gate that got you through the outer office, so I jumped over it. I knocked on his door and respectfully stood before him until he motioned for me to sit down. After a pleasant exchange about Gramp and my time with the volunteers he called over to city hall to verify my position on the list. "How'd the lad do?" were his exact words, as his Irish would have it. He hung up the phone and told me I would be appointed in the order that I had finished and that it would happen before the list ran out. He followed me out of his office and had to show me how to open the latch so I could more gracefully leave.

It soon meant the end of my career at American Hoechst Chemical Corporation and the company got all of five days notice if you count the weekend. Mother in law was more than displeased - dead set against the personal risk I would take for less money. But it was now or never and the economics of the time were all about job security. Carter had beaten Ford because Ford had pardoned Nixon who turned out to be a crook after all. But none of these guys cared enough about working people, choosing instead to follow the money and the perception of power that the scammers and the carpetbaggers promised. We got an energy crisis, rampant inflation, and credit cards to buy what we always used to pay cash out of pocket for. That recession deepened shortly after I was safely employed by the real fire department. They furloughed half of the union help at Hoechst Chemical and almost all of management. Father in law was dismissed altogether and had to move the family all the way to Alabama to find other work. They left Rhode Island forever and almost never came back.

Me and Wife had it made – far and away better than our peers who were graduating college to find no decent jobs. Nothing had come easy but we had made the most of opportunities and it was like we had this big head start on adult life. In other words, we were goddam lucky. Statistically, college graduates were supposed to catch up and zoom on past, but many did not. It was quite an eye opener to learn of how little teachers were paid relative to their education and the crap they had to put up with from everybody else's kids. Other professionals such as mental health and social workers were making even less money than the teachers and they were charged with riding herd on the most dangerous people who weren't locked up. We felt fortunate, secure, blessed. Our healthy young son whom we dearly loved was thriving and we had people around us who really seemed to like having us in the neighborhood. I got to know everybody while Wife kept to herself - wouldn't try to be sociable or even friendly. Her life and her heart would always be in storage somewhere until there was Mastercard - essential to building credit, she said.

By the time the real fire department came calling, we had enrolled the child at Doric Day Pre-school so that we would have day care resolved before me and Wife both had to keep daytime hours at the same time. At first it was for mornings only so that KJ could be acclimated to the idea of other children in his daily life. Kindergarten at Doric Day got to be all day where they got lunch and naps and certified teachers. One was old Mrs. Needham, who I had had for third grade at St. Ann's; made me reconnect with Dad and Miss Valentine. You could drop your kid off as early as you needed to and Mrs. Hersey (who owned the school) would feed your kid supper if it got late enough and she'd even bed him down if need be. Mrs. Hersey lived alone just above the school which was actually a really big house. She had two sons who kept her nicely and without worry. Mr. David was a teacher and Mr. Earl took care of the place and drove the station wagon that served as transportation for the school if you ever needed it. It was a very popular institution with a waiting list of applicants, something like a premium charter school would enjoy. It would take almost all of my part time income to keep my son enrolled there, but it couldn't have been better spent.

Basic training began and there were a number of us who had been volunteer firefighters for quite a while now. Even those that weren't had had firefighting in the military or at least some experience with equipment and machinery. Nobody was helpless and we didn't suffer any mishaps throughout our training with Captain Church. The same guys always drove the ancient fire apparatus that we used in training and the rest of us were happy enough to let them since the old trucks had no synchromesh and no power steering. There were so many of us and so much stuff that when we couldn't get a fire department pickup truck, we used my International so that everything and everybody could go to a site in one trip. If we were burning an old house, for instance, you can't just light one off. You'd have to have regular engine companies present and standing by with lines down off a hydrant and hand lines ready in the event of a miscalculated burn or an apparatus failure or somebody went missing. That also makes for a lot of wet hose to be carried back that the regulars weren't about to handle when there's a collection of rookies to do it.

Churche' – Deputy Chief Ray Church - lived the fire department life and suffered a firefighter's tragic death. But before he was a deputy chief, Churche' was the captain of training and now he was charged with getting 16 people ready for the trucks as quickly as it could be accomplished. He also had to do this pretty much by himself because the city was bare bones for personnel for as long as this economy would last. But they had hired pretty good people when they hired our class – nary a political lackey in evidence. There wasn't a loser in the bunch; no one you couldn't count on, even in their personal lives. None of us ever got pinched or ever got our name in the paper in big letters like some of the politicians should have.

Churche' was one of those old timers who had come up through the Pawtuxet Volunteers in the fifties. You could tell how serious he was by our class photo where he was captured looking away at some skirt that had just come through the door. Churche' didn't hold anything against those of us who were once volunteers like most of the regulars did but it was also understood that once you got on the real fire department, you didn't ride with the volunteers any more. His contemporaries called him "Snack" as in going for a little snack at the Pawtuxet Athletic Club that specialized in 12 ounce curls. If you rode with Snack Church, you didn't just sit in the car and wait for him, either. You went inside and joined him for a cold one and if you didn't, you never got invited again. In those days, the deputies did as they pleased. When Dad moved into the new house at the farm, it cost another deputy his favorite romantic rendezvous at the far end of the driveway. It was a whole other time; red fire trucks, open cabs, and we rode the back step for real.

Churche' was also a working sea captain. He grew up around Pawtuxet Cove and lived on an old wooden cruiser that he covered in plastic for the winter and stayed aboard anyway. It was great how he lived – care free and unavailable for matrimony. He used to talk about the days "when men were men and women were glad of it" and some of the antics that other brass on the job could get real indignant about just made Churche' smile. Churche' had a retirement job lined up to pilot one of the riverboat replicas at Lake Tahoe, but no one could ever imagine the Pawtuxet Cove waterfront without him. Deputy Chief Ray Church collapsed and died in a building fire during the overhaul phase and no one knew it until somebody tripped over the body. His funeral was a spectacular display of fire department tradition; the flag draped casket was carried in the hose-bed of Engine One, his fire boots in reverse on the back step. One of his favorite lines was:

"Wadda ya wanna - live forever?"

Three months of training was compressed into about 3 weeks and soon we were assigned to the trucks where it was assumed that ongoing fireground "evolutions" would complement what we had just learned. My new lieutenant, Al Palumbo, firmly believed that every order, directive, and procedure that came down needed to be fulfilled. I had been assigned to the new station – Station 4 – and the run district was new to everybody and it had to be learned immediately. No such thing as GPS. The "state institutions" was a massive complex of corrections, mental health, and administrative facilities that were difficult by day and impossible at night. Somebody thought it would be a bright idea to wire the new fire alarm system through the bells at Station 4 so that every time a box was pulled, three rounds of "9,9, something, something" would go off. The smoke and heat detectors were also wired in and inmates with nothing else to do learned how to set them off just for our amusement. We spent a lot of time just rewinding the bells.

The bloom fell off of the rose right out of training. I was the rookie – the new guy on our shift - and tradition had it that all the unsavory stuff fell to the rookie. Everybody could tell you what to do and if you objected or complained, it only got worse. Plus, you were on probation for that first year and you didn't dare step off the path. Simple stuff like going to the store or taking the crappiest housework detail was routine as was "traveling". Seniority ruled everything and the bottom guy always got stuck with whatever nobody else wanted, just like at Hoechst. Union rules. Traveling meant that you could be ordered out of assignment to cover a vacancy anywhere else in the city on zero notice and some new guys spent very little time in their home station. That never happened to me because Engine 4 always had to have a 2 man "step" – 2 firefighters plus the officer and driver – but I used to wish that they'd detail me out once in a while. It would have been a vacation from a guy we called "The Spring" who was very publicly exploding about a personal situation not unlike my own. From what I could gather, financial hardship and a rabid lack of self control had put him at odds with his presumptive other half. She wanted him out, gone, dead – whatever it took. He faced losing everything and he wasn't going quietly. His misery spilled over to life at the station and he hated just about everything he laid eyes on. He didn't like me and he didn't think I worked hard enough at being the rookie and he was pretty vocal about it, even to Lieutenant Palumbo. He went so far as to take over my station assignment of cleaning the kitchen because he thought that the stove and refrigerator should be pulled out every day. Lieutenant Palumbo said "Fine – whatever..." and I retreated to the living quarters where I would vacuum all of the rooms and dust everything to a shine, just like I did at home.

One Saturday night a master box came in from a nearby apartment complex followed by a number of "stills". A box alarm alone is more often than not a false alarm simply because pranksters like to pull street boxes. A still alarm is called in by a person who has presumably seen the emergency at hand and a box alarm accompanied by one or more stills is very credible indeed. An apartment complex of this magnitude would also have a fire detection system wired to the fire alarm master box which would identify the building and perhaps even the exact whereabouts of the offended detector .

We pulled up to find smoke billowing out of the main entrance and the actual fire was just inside, in a closet. As Lt. Palumbo jumped out of the truck, he turned to me to yell:

"Stay here 'til I see what we've got!"

Then he dashed inside with the other guy from engine 4 - and no one wearing a Scott*. Meanwhile, the smoke is getting thicker and nobody is moving water, but now I had the time to don a Scott so I grab a booster line* and head in behind them. Everybody's on hands and knees and choking badly on the smoke and they have to get out when I see a fat guy in boxer shorts get dumped on to the hallway floor, dead as they get. My first fatal.

Back at the station I get trashed for doing all the right things that were wrong because they hadn't been ordered by my lieutenant. Never mind that the first requirement is to don a Scott so that you don't become a part of the problem. Nobody did. Never mind that in training you get drilled into bringing in something useful. At least I brought the water to put out the fire, *but I had never been told to*. Enough of this misbehavior as a rookie could cost me my job and everybody thoroughly enjoyed telling me so. Rookie, rookie, rookie – got no rights, no opinion, no say whatsoever.

Seniority and tradition governed everything:

"If you was ever in the service, you'd know these things..."

Every fire station keeps a day sheet to create a record of who's on duty and who's not as well as the active status of each man. Next to your name might be "S" for sick or "O" for occupational injury. Somebody had a little fun with "PG" next to mine for "Probably Going" since there were rumors of a layoff in the wind. I didn't take it all too seriously until the details began to materialize. The city was always in tough shape financially - just one of those circumstances endemic to everywhere in Rhode Island. The C.E.T.A. program (Comprehensive Employment and Training Act) had just been created to offer up federal money to those municipalities who would hire the unemployed. You had to be unemployed for 30 days and then the Fed would pay for the hiring and training for up to a year. Our whole class of 16 was laid off for a month along with four others who had been subsequently added and then hired back under CETA. Nobody would say if it was legal or not - we were just told to shut up about it. The Ford administration never came looking for trouble with a strong Republican mayor and the city couldn't very well close the new station. But 20 salaries paid by the feds for a year? There's no way this deal wasn't going to happen so the union and the city hammered out a tentative agreement that would bring us all back at once. The rest of the job scored a ton of overtime until we returned while I took on a house to paint, took my son fishing, and actually came out ahead.

It was the Hamilton Building fire that decided for me that I would be so much better off on rescue. The structure was this immense and dilapidated wooden affair and it housed the city welfare office where Wife and I had had that one previous experience. The first floor entered from either end of the building through double doors to a vast hallway with offices on each side.

There were a number of layers of false ceilings in each of the two identical levels and the fire had started deep within one of those confines. The first company to arrive was Ladder 3 because Engine 3 was elsewhere and the guys opened fire with what little water they carried. The fire raced across the building before the first engine company ever arrived and by the time we were dispatched on the second alarm, the building was a goner. I had already seen one aberration after another as the fire officers who had been promoted politically could never get it right. On this occasion, we would suck a 30″ water main dry in a vain attempt to suppress the loss that was already a forgone conclusion. Nevertheless, orders flew about as the conflagration grew; one contradiction after another as more and more brass arrived.

Engine 4 and Ladder 2 were dispatched and it was me and Vernon riding the jump seats. Vernon came to us from Engine 10 – a 1500 gallon tanker that we used as a water supply out in the country where there were no hydrants. It was a one man job that was mostly about getting water to the scene but the truck could pump just as well. It was an old man's job, perfectly suited for the guys whose best years were past. The city didn't care about that and in a move to save on personnel, they gave the truck to the volunteers. The four older guys got re-assigned to fill existing vacancies or they retired altogether. Vernon stayed on to become something of a liability on a job where you're either part of the problem or part of the solution. He had his reasons, one being that he had gotten blown off the flight deck of an aircraft carrier during WW II into shark infested waters. He'd tell you about how the hundreds of guys next to him got picked off one by one and how the water was red with blood for hours before he was rescued. At a brush fire, Vernon would empty his Indian can on a hot spot and then sit down next to it until he thought he'd be missed - then he'd emerge for a re-fill. At a house fire, he'd sit on a couch in a smoke filled room until his air ran out - then mosey out for another bottle. When they called for Engine 4 to feed its' own deck gun, Vernon must have thought it would be a good place to sit out the call.

I had already buckled into a Scott when Lt. Palumbo hollered through the cab window for double lines - actually said it twice as he held up two fingers for emphasis. Vernon's immediate reaction was to lean over to me to explain that it had been a while since he'd ever dressed a hydrant with "two over easy". Not to worry, since we had just done it over and over in training and now I knew what my part would be. When we pulled up to the hydrant just east of the building, I let go of the Scott, jumped off the truck, and broke the two lines from the hose bed. As I watched the hose-line pay out, I set about to dress the hydrant. I tried to imagine that there would be enough to reach the building. By the time I made it back to the truck, we had Vernon and half of his fire coat caught up in the rotary gears that move the water cannon and officers screaming to get it in service. The funniest part was when one of the double lines came up short and we didn't have enough water pressure to hit the building.

What wasn't so funny was how close my best friend JB came to being incinerated. He was assigned to Ladder 2 that day with The Spring and they were on the roof cutting vent holes when the evacuation order finally came. On most departments, everyone who hears that order lets loose with siren and air horn - a disjointed orchestration of one long blast that can never be misconstrued. JB had just set foot back on the aerial when the roof caved in. It couldn't have been any closer for him and all because nobody had a clue. There was no chain of command that day - an awful scene where all those senior officers made no sense of the situation whatsoever. Nor would they let it go. Afterwards, they would go from station to station, castigating each company's response in what they labeled "a critique". It ended when The Spring crawled down a deputy's throat that in another era, would have cost him his job.

Mastercard

Just before Wife got caught up in her first indiscretion, Mastercard arrived in our mailbox. Wife had campaigned relentlessly for the convenience of buying without cash or check and apparently decided that she wouldn't be denied by me. I intercepted the first two and made them into little pieces but a truce had to be declared over the third or Nirvana would end. Wife got to shop for stuff that she never even knew we needed and once again there would be no money. Now we could have everything we were willing to make a minimum monthly payment on and soon we had plenty of monthly payment to make. It was much different from American Express, who only charged a reasonable fee in exchange for the convenience of a purchase without cash or check. However, American Express had to be paid in full every month which would have meant that Wife could still only spend what we earned. Mastercard was much less restrained. Revolving credit for the masses soon spun out of control as the balance got bigger and our ability to beat it off diminished. But boy, did we ever have *credit*. Wife was working full time at the bank by now and KJ was in pre-school all day so I started looking for a part time job so we could pay for even more.

Lakewood Hay and Grain was a family held lumber yard and hardware store that began as a feed warehouse in the horse and buggy days. Later they sold coal and other bulk provisions and evolved with the times to survive every form of disaster except the last fire. It was a thriving concern at the time I inquired about a job, and in the beginning I worked there every single day that I wasn't at the station. I had never spent enough time with Gramp at a jobsite to learn much about building construction, but I was immediately available and I was hired as a lumber salesman just the same. Mostly, I took care of walk-in customers - homeowners and contractors alike. Any material that I didn't know about, a lot of these people were happy to explain what it was used for. I loved the job, got along with everyone, and the only down side was about having to be there all the time. My son missed me at home; Wife certainly did not.

I was so angry over the Mastercard debacle that I took over the checkbook and paid all the bills myself. If I was going to have to work all these goddam hours, these bills were gonna get paid by my hand alone and there would be accountability for all the crap we now owned. Imagine my surprise when the Mastercard bill was returned along with the check that was judged to be illegible. They said that because they couldn't decipher my official signature, they were rejecting payment. I re-wrote the check and sent it back to Mastercard and when the next statement came, they had assessed us a late charge. When Wife got home from the bank that night I tore into her purse and cut the card to shreds. I was working 80 hours a week because I had to and now even lunch money came hard. Wife responded by serving up her despicable tuna noodle casserole which I promptly hummed out the back door. We were at serious odds.

Wife began once again with the same Twogae she had dallied with before marriage. Wife had a little frustration of her own to manage but she couldn't do it alone and she wouldn't enlist her husband except to assault him with it. The way she wanted to justify it, she and the Twogae had seized upon a moment of readiness and it would never happen again until the next time. Wife said that if I wanted to, then I could just go have a time of my own and she wouldn't mind one bit - that I was entitled - as though we were trading goddam energy credits. I knew the problem from the beginning since Wife hadn't come complete with an apparent libido and we had to feel our way along for it the way youngsters are supposed to. Relative inexperience never seemed to stop other people from trying and from loving just the same and even the Catholics would agree that you should discover each other together. You were only supposed to be afraid of it *before* marriage. "I do" was supposed to mean "we will" on each and every front except that it didn't for us. Instead there was anger, insult, sorrow and in the end, very little forgiveness. We had been to a counselor - one of those Master's & Johnson disciples. After a few sessions where we each got to complain about the other, the counselor met with us individually. He told me rather directly that my wife did not love me, probably never had, and certainly never would. He said that he really couldn't help us and that he wouldn't take any more of our money. That more or less settled it. I didn't love her either, although I had always wanted to. I tried to move on from the affair and Wife did not and nothing wanted to improve. Although Wife implied that she still wanted a husband, I had somehow gotten myself disqualified. It was a blue collar soap opera through and through, where all that was missing was a felony.

Whenever Wife wasn't unhappy, she was downright miserable. She had been torn from a happy mid-west teenage life and dragged to another world where she had nothing to call her own until she had me and KJ thrust upon her. The obvious upside was that she gained her freedom from her mother's overbearing catholicism and she got to have her chance at middle class American life. It would never be enough. Love had never joined us with each other - only with our son. Still, we trudged on as a family. We went places and did things and appearances mattered but I would look forward to my nights at the fire station a lot more than ever. Leave my troubles at the door and go be the hero I knew for sure that I was, at least for the night. When Wife later announced that she had conceived a Twogae, it was almost apparent that this ride needed to be over.

Wife opted for curettage and about a pound of prevention and I had to sign off as the husband of record. I suppose I could have gallantly offered to raise another man's progeny but it was catholic enough that I nursed Wife through yet another blood clot so that she could soon choose to be on her way. One of her sisters was with us by now, just finishing up at URI since the in-laws had already moved. She helped out by looking after KJ so that I could be everywhere else but if she'd have winked, I'd have nodded. Wife had indeed said that I was entitled.

1949

Just before the conflagration between me and soon to be ex-Wife, I met Ivory Marr. Mr. Marr was 88 years old and he was one of these old time builders who came into the lumber yard once in a while looking for "just the right bawwd". He still had a few customers who would never hire anybody else and he was so old and alone that he never saw himself doing anything else. Sort of like Gramp, although Gramp and Mr. Marr never knew each other. Mr. Marr drove a sparkling blue 67' Malibu 2 door hard-top that was beautifully kept and when I was talking to Larry Doughty about it, he told me about the old Dodge pick-up that Mr. Marr wanted to sell. Larry was just out of high school and he worked with me at Lakewood Hay&Grain almost like a partner. He was hot for "little Irene" who used to stroll by and she knew it but she ended up getting the crap beat out of her by someone else who didn't love her so much. Larry would have been a much better choice.

The truck was a red and black 1949 Dodge B1B pick-up that had MARR CONSTRUCTION stenciled on the door along with a "3" right under the fuel neck. It was a cold February night during a snowfall that I got to see how well Mr. Marr had kept this truck – in a garage. It hadn't been run in a long time but Mr. Marr was adamant that it would start right up. Mr. Marr was a true Colonial from Vermont; he once fired an ancient flintlock at a burglar and the ball nearly split a tree in half in his back yard. Vermont shares a dialect with Maine and sheep:

"I've gaat the batry ovuh heeyaa.."

Larry had told me that the Dodge had a rod knockin'; maybe

two so I didn't need to fire it up and I certainly didn't want to do it in the cold. These old flatheads are known for their soft bottom ends and I didn't want a rod letting go. I pulled the dipstick to find thick black sludge and down a quart so that pretty much confirmed that we really shouldn't run this truck in the cold.

"Whaat, ya dun't want tuh heaah-it run?"

I offered Mr. Marr a deposit against the $200.00 that he wanted but he declined - said I could pay him when I came for the truck. A week or so later me and Louie Fontaine went over with the International and dragged it home.

Wife was less than pleased but I was happy enough to have something to look forward to doing out in the driveway. Me and KJ took the whole truck apart and stored it all in the tool shed except for the cab and the frame. We got all of his neighborhood friends and anybody else who wanted to help and gave them each some sandpaper. A couple of gallons of Kool-Aid later, the frame and four steel wheels were ready for paint. I took the sheet metal parts to the station where I wound The Spring right up as I set about to strip the paint and Lt. Palumbo said it was O.K. The engine went to Simplex Automotive where the only hold-up was a bad crankshaft. We found a good one at Greasy Joe's junkyard and soon the motor came back brand new. When Wife left us, the truck was still at Cranston Auto Body being painted and I had to get a loan to finish it. Then me and KJ took it to Davy Jones - "The Pinstriper" - famous throughout Rhode Island for his freehand style. Will Park who owned Cranston Auto Body told me to show up at Davy's house at nine o'clock sharp on any Saturday morning with an 8 – pack of Miller stubbies so we could be first in line. It was a marvel to watch this guy; a true artistic performance. He'd take a stubbie between thumb and forefinger right at the top of the neck, take a short swig, and then lay down a perfect line for as long as it needed to go. It was almost like he held out the stubbie for ballast. He'd do this over and over until he was satisfied that there was just enough - that the truck wasn't over done. When I asked him to sign his work, Davy seemed a little hesitant - as though no one ever thought to ask. Then he drew a little paintbrush on the lower right corner of the tailgate and signed it "Style by Jones". There was a sign painter who used to come into Lakewood Hay & Grain. Will Park had done such a nice job of finishing the truck – even fabricated new running boards – that I hired this guy to paint:

"CRANSTON AUTO BODY"

on the sideboards the same way Gramp had done with his trucks. Will had heard about this from a mutual friend and when I stopped in to see him one day, he grinned:

"Thanks for bringing back my truck."

Mr. Marr had had his prostate out so he wasn't moving beyond his front porch when I went to see him. I had just put the truck on the road and I was so sure that he would just swell with pride over what I had done to his truck. He liked it well enough but one day he came into the lumberyard when I wasn't there and said to the guys:

"That gawd dam fool spent ovuh fourteen hunnert dahlahs
on a truck I only paid twelve hunnert fer!"

We're on our third "hunnert" thousand miles.

Snakebite

"Mommy, when are you coming home?"

"Your father won't let me come home"

Stunned; my heart fluttered and I wished that just this once, she would drop stone cold dead on the floor. At that very moment nothing else mattered because like I know my name, I knew what those words would mean forever. There was no fix; nothing that could be said that would yield any measure of comfort for a little boy who desperately missed his mother at home. He cried for her constantly yet he managed a day to day existence that didn't seem to hold me responsible for her absence. He couldn't accept that she had chosen to leave but he also knew that I had asked her not to. We had been separated a while and now she had come to pick KJ up and take him for the night and apparently she had made some plans. We had just gotten home and I had him in the tub when she arrived and she was none too pleased that he wasn't ready to go. Bath time was supposed to be fun but for now, we just had to get it done. No need for a scene; keep a little composure for the child and just get them out the door.

"YOU WON"T LET MY MOMMY COME HOME!!!"

There had been no discussion about reconciliation. Wife had said only one time that she wanted to come back but she was honest enough to admit that it was much more a matter of security for her than about us as an item. Friends with benefits, but only for one. Wife had no money, an armload of bills and an apartment in a fire trap a few blocks from a neighborhood that you wouldn't want your kids to know. She wanted the comfort of home and hearth but she had grown accustomed to the attention and the affectations that the licentiousness of the era – indeed of any era – had always produced. Wife had said that she needed to move on and "find herself" and that I would be more qualified to keep custodial care of our child, in our home, as long as I would share. She in turn would come and stay on nights that I had to be at the station and we would always put the welfare of our child first. Visitation didn't even have to be spelled out - "such time as the parties mutually agree to" said the decree. We'd be so mature - maybe even be friends once again. A smooth transition, a perfect dissolution; perhaps even have drinks and dinner together like those couples on TV. But I had been to see the lawyer where I had to listen to myself describe out loud how the guy who was supposed to be re-modeling my bathroom had re-entered my wife instead. I got angry all over again and I never wanted her back. Me and KJ would move on, all by myself.

I was on Rescue 3 with Budlong and a bunch of other terrific guys on the 1st Platoon. The fire department schedule consists of two ten hour days followed by two fourteen hour nights followed by four days off. It is a terrific shift to be a firefighter, especially if the truck sleeps all night. Six days in a row and six nights in a row - off. If you're ambitious you can accomplish a lot, especially if you're "out the door for four"; four days in a row off. Or you could have a whole other full time job like I did at Lakewood Hay&Grain. The guys at the lumber yard took my news in stride since someone had seen Wife out and about and everybody knew what would only be a matter of time. I reduced my hours at the lumber yard during the week and quit weekends altogether so that I could be more than the parent who always had to get his kid somewhere else. Once this new life was up and running, it wasn't half bad after the anxiety subsided. He'd stop crying for his mother eventually, right? Just wait this thing out until he was so busy at life that mommy wouldn't matter. Keep him occupied, satisfied - sanctify myself right before his eyes. Just keep being the dad he'd always known - hell, she was the one who left so *she* was *the one* to *blame*. Yes, let's go with that - for a child who wasn't yet four. And don't let his mommy come home.

Battle stations weren't really manned until after a couple of volleys went unanswered. Wife now had the social life that she had so missed out on and nobody to answer to. She never drank much or did drugs so she never had intoxicants to blame - always of her own mind did she decide. The first time Wife needed to excuse herself from overnight duty set off a firestorm because I wasn't having it and I laid it right down that her child care responsibilities were not negotiable. Wife laid it down right back that if I wanted her continued cooperation then I had better learn to handle some of these exceptions. And too bad if I didn't like that silver Mercedes that was parked in my driveway; who she sees is none of my business and he doesn't stay over, anyway. So I said right back that Wife could expect to have no child at Christmas if she couldn't be more dependable and keep that guy *out of my house!* Back and forth it went until we traded final insults and she left in a rage.

Sometime after, Mom called to inquire. We had been to visit Gram and Gramp and Mom must have caught an earful about just how alone we were. Dad was still upside down over not being in charge of everybody and you could feel the hesitation in Mom trying not to say the wrong thing. She didn't speak for Dad but she said that if she could help, she'd like to.

"Why the sudden interest?"
"Because this needs to stop"

I eventually found myself turning into their driveway and KJ was reunited with his "Mona". Dad was sensible enough to act with indifference and I was happy enough with détente. I might still need these people after all.

The year that Wife's family left the area, Wife's brother transferred from UCONN to URI. He was too independent and too broke for dorm life so he lived in a wooden camper perched on the back of an old GMC pickup that he moved around the parking lot until he was invited to leave by campus security. When Wife's sister left, Brian asked to stay with us until he could make other arrangements. After Wife left, Brian was invited to stay on. Brian commuted back and forth to URI on a bright orange Honda 350 in a bright orange helmet and when the weather turned foul, he bought a one piece waterproof flight suit and drove through monsoon and blizzard alike. Then he'd be home and I could go out later and my son wouldn't even know I was gone. Brian was never any trouble and he was welcome for as long as he wanted to stay and it didn't even matter that he was Wife's brother. Life finally settled down to a routine that no one complained about except that husband and soon to be ex-Wife openly hated each other - me more than her. Any hopes I had ever had of living happily ever after with my little boy and the woman of my dreams would have to wait for another woman. I would be the new single dad, making the decisions and the choices and sometimes the sacrifices that would be important to raising my son. To my way of thinking, I was entirely justified, qualified and authentic. I would keep my son warm and safe and dry and fed. I was so proud of how I would keep us; TV couldn't have gotten it any better.

Doric day School was an ongoing expense and Wife didn't help a whole lot because she was always destitute and needed to keep herself current for work and dating and such. Anything that she did buy always had to go back to her place - clean and folded if I didn't mind - so that KJ would have something fresh to wear and so Wife could keep an eye on her investiture. There would be no child support; nothing asked and nothing ever offered. Wife could have anything she could carry away as long as I could keep the house for our son to grow up in and she took everything that would fit into her new digs. I was left with the living room sofa because no one would help her move it, the liberty bell lamps that she no longer deemed a "must have", and a bare box spring and mattress that Wife's sister had left behind upstairs. Wife took the new Datsun and burned up the motor when she ran it out of oil but I imagine Mastercard paid for the repair. My old Dodge truck was still at Cranston Auto Body being painted and all I had to drive was the International – not exactly a chick magnet. I snagged a Chevy Impala that had no rear brakes to drive in the interim and it had no rear brakes when I finally sold it. I knew I would have a few bills coming at me so I took out a payroll deductible loan at our employee credit union to render myself solvent once again - and to pay the lawyer.

The attorney was Al Ciullo who sat patiently and listened curiously to my tale of sainthood. I explained what soon to be exWife and I had agreed to and he was astounded that I thought this would all go as simply as I had laid it out. Mr. Ciullo added that the property settlement agreement should be entered into Superior Court where it would be enforced as a contract rather than as a Family Court decree. This would entitle neither party to revisit any of the hard assets that had been agreed to and that exWife would have no further claim on the house. We hadn't owned the house long enough to compile much equity, so it could be clearly demonstrated that exWife would be getting much more of value from the deal. That didn't stop her from complaining long and loud later on.

The process in Rhode Island is far from simple when it comes to getting somebody's name off a property. A "quit claim" is filed where said property passes through a number of hands before it can be yours alone. It requires that you partner with someone you trust entirely because that person also becomes a legal owner of record for a while. I asked Gramp first off because he was honorable and trustworthy and the patriarch of our clan. Gramp was reluctant because of his age, fearing that his death would create a hardship for me and for his own estate and he told me to enlist Dad.

"Whatsamatter with your father?" he asked.

I replied directly that I would not use Dad, that I would never give Dad that kind of stranglehold over my affairs. I work in a dangerous profession and I also have an estate to consider. It was probably the first time Gramp ever thought about just how aggrieved it was between me and Dad because this was not a trivial matter. Gramp reluctantly agreed to do this for me and the process took a year, but it went smoothly. I don't know if Dad ever found out about it, but I hope so.

When we finally went to court, we got the hangin'est judge of them all. Judge Goldberg had a reputation for going right at dads who didn't pay their child support or who otherwise defied orders from the Family Court. He'd put you right in jail, right then and there. We got to watch some of this before it was our turn and it's enough to make your little heart go pit – a – pat. Guys got yelled at and hauled off and their lawyers got admonished for wasting the court's time. Judge Goldberg seemed to get angrier as the morning wore on, and then it was our turn. I was confident that we had everything in order and my two witnesses had arrived but as we sat down, Mr. Ciullo quietly whispered:

"Take a breath; we're not out this yet."

"HUH?"

"This is Family Court – the judge says what goes.
She can still change her mind about everything."

The "I"s were dotted and the "T"s were crossed and we were in complete agreement about everything and now it could all just disintegrate. Soon to be exWife sat alone looking about as vulnerable as a puppy when Judge Goldberg asked her directly about being without counsel. She answered just as directly that she needed no counsel, that everything was fine by her. Judge Goldberg asked her once again, even offering to appoint someone to represent her and still, she held her own. When Judge Goldberg asked her about leaving behind sole custody of her son, of leaving the domicile of her own free will, she replied honestly enough in the affirmative. There was a chilling exchange when Budlong, who was one of my witnesses failed to be audible and the judge impatiently told him twice to speak up.

"I am speaking up" he growled

There was a moment of dread that the wheels could come off at this instant but everybody kept their composure and suddenly, we were out of there. Budlong nailed exWife the following night.

Cranston Rescue

Ronald Sterling Jones was the Deputy Chief when I was first assigned to Platoon 2, Engine 4, right out of training. He had been the training officer before Churche' and he had a particular penchant for Rescue. Chief Jones and Captain Richard Brown were among the pioneers of the modern rescue service in Rhode Island in general and Cranston in particular. They had been trying all along to improve upon the dismal results of resuscitation in the field with some of the most barbaric equipment ever invented. They once used a crude defibrillator that employed saline soaked pads and it ran on AC power from a wall outlet. Capt. Brown used to talk about the tingle you could get if you were touching anything close to the patient and there was a real danger of electrocution. In those days, "CLEAR!" meant "clear the room".

In Cranston, scoop and run gave way to an "a la carte" approach to advanced life support in the field. State of the art lost out to fiscal reality so there would never be a nationally accredited paramedic program but inroads were made just the same. One by one, procedures and medications and equipment were added and patients arrived at ER's more properly treated and breathing. It took a while to get area physicians on board and there were some isolated turf wars but the general public had been so well educated by the TV show "Emergency", there was no stopping it. The politicians could never make a credible excuse for failing to support real life-saving measures and after an armload of pressure from the League of Women Voters, they found the money to get it started. Initially, there were two hospitals and two respective physicians dedicated to getting this program off the ground - Dr. Capone of Rhode Island Hospital and Dr. Lamb from Kent County Memorial. Later there would be Dr. Kaye from The Miriam Hospital and Dr. Conrad from South County Memorial. None of this could have been accomplished without the innumerable coronary care nurses instructing those of us who would administer to a critically ill patient. The state created an EMS office and a medical director and initially, we all operated under the authority and direction of a single MD license. Once this got started, the real fire department all but abandoned the new and improved rescue service. The old timers wanted nothing to do with "the doctor truck" so right off the bat it turned into a young man's game. We got to put the new face on a division that hadn't changed much since the undertakers had it.

I had been leaning towards a career in rescue almost from the time I joined the real fire department. Just a few years before, Mr. Curtis - the scoutmaster - collapsed at the historic Sprague Mansion where we were all working at cleaning up the grounds as a joint Boy Scout service project. Mr. Curtis never took another breath once he hit the ground and all the Boy Scout first aid we thought we were so good at was worthless. So was Cranston Rescue at the time. The two guys who showed up acted like this was not a serious situation at all and they took their sweet time "rushing" Mr. Curtis off to the hospital. There was no such thing as advanced life support; no such thing as CPR. I played "Taps" for Mr. Curtis at his funeral; now I wanted for us to do so much better.

Three out of the four Deputy Chiefs' would get you hurt or killed on the fire line just through sheer incompetence. I had been to a number of general alarm fires up to then and we never achieved anything but total loss. None of the deputies ever thought to bust a hole for ventilation and indeed, it was discouraged – like it was a sign of defeat if you ever had to cut a hole in the roof. Even at the Hamilton Building fire, ventilation was an afterthought while guys were taking a beating inside. No one ever actually *said* that stupid was a bona fide fire department tradition but guys just did as they were told and fires vented themselves until all that was left was the cellar. At the Hamilton Building fire, I was one of the guys deep within the inferno when the 2-1/2" attack line went limp. When I added that to all the other stupid that went on, I wanted rescue even more.

I got through all of the training O.K. with a lot of mentoring from Hawkins who was in charge of Rescue 2 on my shift. Hawk was the epitome of cool, calm, collected and he had zero use for stupid but he was patient with me just the same. He'd just smile when I called him old, like how can your back be that bad at 30? I'd have my day, he said, and he hoped to be around when I did. The following year, I went down pretty hard and by the time I was 30, I was in worse shape than Hawk. Injury accompanies a job where all the heavy-weights live three floors up and especially when we have to move out in a hurry. You can't always plant those feet and lift with your legs and you can't always wait for more help to arrive, so you just do whatever it takes. The trade-off for me was the independence that rescue enjoys. The truck could come and go at will - out of sight and out of the minds of the rest of the department who couldn't care less what we were doing.

I spent most of my career on Rescue 3 at Station 1 in Edgewood – the east side of Cranston that sits along Narragansett Bay between Providence and Warwick. Prior to the new Station 4 and the new Rescue 3, the original rescue companies ran alternately as Rescue 1 and Rescue 2 out of Station 2 headquarters in the center of the city. Now that they had assigned Rescue 2 to the new station 4 in Garden City, Edgewood could no longer count on immediate response if Rescue 1 was out. Edgewood had always been the seat of Republican power in Cranston and now these old time politicos weren't about to be denied. The same thinking mayor who had secured the CETA money and who had insured the city buildings so they could safely burn also scored some DOT money to build the new Rescue 3. The new rescue would be the first "modular" rescue truck the fire department had ever purchased and because it was DOT money, it had to be white with orange marking. This upset the old timers who would never even accept the recent change to yellow, but any color other than traditional red was unacceptable to them, anyway. More stupid tradition, but try to move them off it - can't be done.

Rescue 3 was fabricated onto a 1976 Ford F-350 chassis and the electrical alone must have taken a month to complete. But modular it was with cabinet space for everything, a connected avenue from cab to patient compartment and a side escape door that today is the law. The truck was built by a local company that won the bid purely on the specifications of being a serious Republican donor. We got lucky because they were also the best local outfit for the job. The guys who had been on rescue awhile were allowed serious input and we got everything we wanted in the truck. We didn't get to keep it in Edgewood for very long, however. Rescue 1 out ran us about 4:1 and their vehicle needed to be retired and junked. Instead, the brass traded trucks with Edgewood and we mostly shut up and lived with it until our run count got established.

Initially Rescue 3 was a very sheltered existence because the first due run district wasn't very big and the truck usually slept all night. But nearby Providence had only 3 rescue companies where they needed at least 5 and soon we were unofficially Providence Rescue 4 by way of the very official mutual aid agreement. I was assigned to Steve Budlong who was happy enough that I seemed to know everything but he would have been just as happy if I had kept it to myself. We were friends forever but we weren't partnered for long. After they created the rank of Rescue Lieutenant, all of the rescue driver jobs were made available by seniority to the older rescue guys who hadn't passed the test. A lot of them went back to an engine or a ladder company, but another guy took my job with Budlong (who did get promoted) and I got bumped back to Garden City. After a short miserable stint on Rescue 2, I bid to the third platoon to be with Lieutenant Pelico and remained there until he retired.

Brand new to rescue, I was also working part time 40 hours at the lumberyard. KJ was at Doric Day Pre-school where they also taught an accredited kindergarten all day instead of the usual half. KJ thrived at Doric Day from the very first and Mrs. Hersey offered us every consideration whenever I got a late call or a fire held us over. She was very offended about the idea of a mother leaving her child and she knew what I was up against. One day I was working off shift when, just prior to my relief at shift change, we got called to the school. I knew that there would only be a few kids at that hour and I prayed that this call wouldn't be about mine. We still hadn't been very well educated in pediatric care - just basic life support - and we mostly treated children as "little adults". I ran in to find KJ passed out on the floor, burning with fever. I was with Mike Krieg who was also an LPN and a field medic in Vietnam and he took immediate charge. After a few cold compresses KJ came around a little and I didn't throw up with fear. In the ER at Roger Williams Hospital they saw him right away and did a spinal tap to rule out the meningitis that was going around at the time. It turned out to be a virus that spiked a big enough temp that can cause a convulsion in some kids. Shook me a little, though.

Driving Rescue is about the closest I would ever come to driving NASCAR. The law gives license to play dodge-em' through the gauntlet of cross town Park Avenue a little faster than the posted speed and some of us were more brazen than others. It could be exhilarating but on advice of counsel, contact with the motoring public should be avoided. There was no formal training, no written rules to govern our behavior behind the wheel other than what the officer would tolerate. We served something of an apprenticeship where you learned from experience about what the truck could or could not do. Making it go was the easy part and I didn't slow down any until I put Lt. Budlong down hard in the back of the truck. We were transporting an elderly woman and had just gotten under way when I hit a sharp dip in the road and the truck bottomed out. The equal and opposite reaction brought a scream out of the old lady and when I stopped to investigate, Budlong was flat on his back with her on top of him. It would have been hilarious if Steve wasn't so PO'ed and for the rest of the day I got to trade places while he drove. The motion alone was enough to flip my stomach but Budlong knew some even better moves that would cure me of reckless driving forever.

Soon there got to be a whole new world of women within and without the medical field. I had never been a part of the club scene but Disco had taken hold and guys got dragged into it kicking and screaming. I found an edge by getting on the list for paid overtime gigs at a place called "Bogart's" that was so crowded that they required a fire department detail in uniform. Bogart's had this bad practice of locking the exits because people would let their friends in to beat the cover charge. Management would actually chain the panic bars together, relying on some half - assed security (read bouncers) to get them open in the event of a stampede. Fire departments everywhere had learned otherwise from the 1942 Cocoanut Grove fire in Boston and more recently, the Beverly Hills Supper Club fire that killed 165 people. This wasn't going to happen while I was in charge and when management wouldn't cooperate, I'd call the duty deputy. Bogart's only needed to be closed down once on my watch.

Bogarts was a great detail. You got time and a half to watch the exits, check the fire extinguishers, and infatuate women. Another great detail was any function at Rhodes on the Pawtuxet, a gigantic venue from the Gatsby era that sits on the Pawtuxet River just upstream from Narragansett Bay. They could accommodate hundreds if not thousands of people and served every imaginable function - ballroom dancing, high school proms or formal banquets. They even had professional boxing. In olden days, you could rent a rowboat there on a Sunday afternoon and paddle your sweetie all about the river. The ballroom alone must cover half an acre of hardwood floor and there are upstairs balconies where you could get a little cozy or very lost. The place is so big that if it ever burns, they'll see it from the Space Station. Management cooperated fully, preferring us to be mostly out of sight, and you could get free drinks at the end of the shift. It was another great place to hook up if you were trolling and when the fire department uniform went from military khakis to blues, you could own the room.

There had to be a first carnal escapade postWife and BellaDonna was an intoxicating foray into the netherworld of intimacy that I had so longed for. I met her through Hawkins who said she was very fair in word and deed and well worth getting to know. Having been stifled by exWife for all those years, it was hard to believe that desire from another could become so unleashed. "Friends first" had no place in this torrent of unrestrained passion and lust. We were good enough to each other in so many ways that when we parted, the relationship was left open to renewal at another time.

I thought I had a shot with a girl named Denise who worked at the hardware store at Lakewood Hay&Grain. She had always liked me before Wife became exWife which is to say she was friendly and she smiled a lot. She had long thick ebony hair and emerald green eyes but before I could be single, she was betrothed. No surprise there. Then there were the twins who worked at Cranston General Hospital and some others who worked at Roger Williams Hospital but in the beginning, no one ever clicked and some just said no. Frigid; perhaps even man-haters, I thought until I learned that intelligent, professional, independent women mostly don't give themselves over without some consideration. A woman needs a reason; a guy just needs a place. I took up with some good enough women, discarded others, and helped myself to as much sin as the next guy.

Lizzy was a peanut of a nurse in the ER at Rhode Island Hospital. She was my very first formal date post-Wife and her "friends first" rule never got past "friends only". She lived in a swanky Providence hi-rise and drove a hot little MG that actually ran pretty well where most did not. We hung out - never so much as a hard kiss - but she took me all over the city and offered up a few clues about how to better approach the softer gender. I had never met a gay guy couple, but Liz knew a pair - a Laurel&Hardy look-alike where the skinny guy was quiet and shy and always looked like he was about to cry. "Oh, but don't they *swish*" she'd say after they had left. We would both go on to lose ourselves in other toxic loves but we were pals and we kept each other sane. She drank Campari and soda and she smoked long Kools and she introduced me to Tangueray over just plain gin. We used to bar - hop the upper east side of Providence as well as some of the dingiest places where she would never dare to go alone. We shopped for shoes, cooked for each other and spent a Christmas together with the gay guys when neither of us had anybody to be with. For a long time Liz Truitt was my best friend and my only comfort. KJ even liked her.

Me and KJ had three different breakfast haunts that he could choose from every weekday before school but dinner was always at home. I had learned to cook in the kitchens I had worked over the years and the fire station offered up even more culinary adventures. We always had a Crock Pot and I could put together a stew or some meatballs the night before and then just zip home from the lumberyard at noon to plug it in. Brian would eat with us whenever he was around and so would Liz so it couldn't have been too bad - certainly better than any tuna noodle casserole. You'd never find Hamburger Helper or any of that other pre-fabricated crap in my house either and I made soups, breads and desserts as well. Rusty always got some of what was left and he never complained either.

I had three separate rounds with redBeth at a time when I really thought I was looking for something stable and she wanted anything but. To say that opposites attract would mostly define this unholy union and no one either before or since has rocked my swagger the way redBeth did. Beth was cute and pert and clever and funny but mostly she was red-headed and not serious or giving at all. I fell in love with the red-headed part, took it all to my very heart and wanted desperately to make her my own because I couldn't. Seems I was so accustomed to shoveling sand against the tide that I didn't know how to stop; didn't want to. It ended forever only when redBeth announced that she just didn't have it for me and couldn't foresee it ever happening. She was emphatic enough that I wondered why she had ever bothered with me at all. Liz said she didn't see anything there either and that redBeth would be a hard one to hold on to.

I had other help. My friend Robin had very definite views about what honesty should entail and if there were insurmountable issues, a bad match should end sooner rather than later. Who needs all that sexual tension? A guy's dream, a guy's view - Rob so totally gets it; the kind of honesty we all think we want. Too bad she was already taken. She'll look right at you and tell you anything else you need to know about a cut-the-crap relationship. From her refreshing point of view, life is just too short to be restrained by traditional values or the judgment or the baggage of others. Love happens or it doesn't; why not live well just the same? Robin could never get just *what the hell* I was doing with redBeth - said I was nuts, wasting myself like that. So now that's two smart women who cared enough about me to say out loud what everybody else must have been thinking. Given the level of high anxiety, a developing ulcer, and a child at home, I finally had to quit going the extra mile for someone who would never go my way. I went down for the third time and never went back for more. Me and KJ just kept doing what we did, day in and day out. We were almost fine.

I got shuffled around on Rescue trucks for a time since I had almost no seniority and the promotions made a lot of people move. I finally got to settle in on the third platoon in Edgewood with Lt. Louie Pelico and I'd still be there with him if it were up to me. Louie and I had a great time and no fear and we worked on a shift that was nicknamed "the radical third". Even the deputy was a mover - had girlfriends all over the city and played guitar in an old timer's combo. It was the 70's and before there was AIDS there were women who came calling at all hours for guys we all knew but wouldn't identify. There was weed but not at the station and alcohol was a much bigger problem. Our guys who didn't have to drag themselves to work were mostly O.K. and we always managed to cover for the others until they either straightened out or did themselves in. We had to keep Saugy and one of the deputies a little oiled though, or they couldn't function at all. For our part, me and Louie stayed clean out of trouble. Everybody liked Louie and I was straighter than straight on the outside so we got to fly under the radar a little. There were rumors about activities at the station in Edgewood that even the cops were watching. It had either all run its' course before I arrived or it was well hidden from my view since I was new. Shady characters came and went and loose women were everywhere but I can't say I ever saw anything ever happen that the law would frown upon. And Louie would say the same, for the record.

Louie picked up on my sorry self where Robin left off and we got to be great friends. He saw me losing sleep and weight over redBeth and talked some Robin sense into me and added a little of his own. When "no" means no, its' always going to mean "no" and didn't I leave off with exWife for much of this very same? In a world full of promising amusement peeking out of every corner, why would I want to keep putting myself away? I was 26.

Summer of Love

The guys who owned the Arbi restaurant where I used to work bought what was once "Maria's" on Park Avenue and renamed it "The Arbi Inn". The place was especially famous for the gangland execution of Louis "The Fox" Taglianetti and his unfortunate mistress. The fire made it even more so.

It was bitter cold in February when Engine 2 pulled up around midnight to what started out as a smoke condition. Once again, the deputy wouldn't open the roof and the truck was a little too close when the front window blew out. Fire lines were already feeding Engine 2 which also had men and lines in the building so the truck couldn't be easily moved. Ladder 2 immediately set up a water curtain to protect the truck and soon everything was ice. We fought this fire from behind the curve throughout and effectively saved the cellar. They filled the hole, paved it over, and rented it to Matt Olerio as an open air produce stand. The following year they raised the rent on this parking lot beyond what Matt was willing to pay so Matt moved into a regular store where he also seemed to do pretty well. Me and my brother Steven grabbed up the lot thinking that we'd do even better than Matt since Dad had the farm and we could get most of our produce from him on the cheap. Dad was still mostly indifferent to me but he'd help Steven if he could help himself as well. We'd get rich and I could leave the lumberyard behind forever if I wanted to. Dad felt otherwise and instead, we found ourselves paying regular price while Dad saved himself the trouble of taking his produce to market because Steven would just bring it with him in the big GMC we had bought to haul everything else with. What we didn't get from Dad, we had to buy at the regular farmer's market in Providence so me and KJ would take the old Dodge and get there early for some of the good stuff. We'd go to breakfast and then back to the market to buy some of what was getting older by the minute so we could sell it in volume as a special. Then we'd meet Steven at the stand and decide how to manage the day.

School was out so KJ spent time with Mom at the farm if I had to be at the station or he could stay with us at the stand and help out. During the week me and Steven could trade afternoons off when it was slow so I could still always take a truck load of kids and Rusty swimming at Curran Reservoir or the Trench. It was mostly a summer of running exhaustively in place because it got us almost nowhere. The weather failed to cooperate; it rained on every Friday and Saturday, the prime shopping days. Since all we could shelter was the produce, people just drove on by. We sold grapes out of a cooler and watched people shake the bunches so that our profit could fall off the vine. We had to padlock our dumpster to keep other stuff out including the scavengers who drove nice cars. I kept my single round of double aught on the floor of the Jimmy since we also carried a lot of cash. Everything except the big wooden vegetable bins went with us when we closed for the day, leaving little of value to vandals. After we paid the rent, the dumpster, and part-time Suzi (who later married David), there was very little left. Liz told everybody at the hospital about our produce stand and brought in all of her friends and that helped us a lot. Fire department wives came in also and even redBeth had to satisfy her curiosity.

Right across the street was a little convenience store where me and Steven would duck in to cool off or get a drink. The manager was a nineteen year old blonde Mensa wannabe with a perfect face and a better body who agreed to let us keep some of our perishables in the walk-in fridge overnight. She lived nearby and her disaffected boyfriend used to take her to work but not anymore. It was a long enough walk to make her late sometimes so I offered to pick her up on my way. This led to morning coffee with her mom who was red and less than 40 and she sat right across from me in almost nothing to wear. There were two other sisters who were younger than Mensa and they didn't bat an eye at any of this. There were no men of the household but little Bethany wanted one and she really wanted it to be me. That got a little complicated right after Mensa took really good care of everything I imagined we might do together. Former boyfriend re-assessed and reappeared, knowing full well that what he didn't want to lose forever seemed to be getting away. Mensa had made her point and I was glad to help but I really wish I had moved on her mom instead.

It had ended with redBeth and I hadn't gotten over it when suddenly we found ourselves face to face in the ER and she agreed to take up with me once again. I wanted nothing more than to bring her in from the cold to be with me and KJ, figuring that once I warmed her up, we'd catch fire. That obsession once again took hold while I remained oblivious that redBeth had yet to consider what someone other than herself might require.

Rod Stewart was coming to the Providence Civic Center and he was hot as a pistol back then and redBeth loved him. I ran right down to the box office and bought the best seats available so I could surprise redBeth. The very next day, redBeth decreed once again that I should no longer be in love with her. Smitten with redBeth no longer, I went down to the Civic Center on the night of the concert and sold my perfect seats to a couple of girls who were last in line, hoping to get lucky at a sold out show. They had about half of the cost between them and I took a little less so they could get a soda. It made me feel so much better that I went over to our firefighter's club and kept it going for a while longer. I don't know how I got home.

"Linda 2" was a vanity plate on a '65 Rambler that I came to know as a death defying ride. The driver was a statuesque Marilyn Monroe look-alike who worked at the IMH* as a keeper of the crazy and her favorite pastime was fisticuffs with the clientele. One evening, she took the worst of it to her ribcage for a little summer time off and me and Felix took her to the ER in the old pre-modular Rescue 2. She was so game that she insisted on riding up front with us instead of laid out in the back and she told us dirty jokes all the way to the hospital. Felix handed off the info for me to make out the run report but I wouldn't - it was his job as the Lieutenant.

"You sure?" he said as he held up the pad.

I looked a little closer at what he had written, and he *had gotten her phone number!*

"Gimme that!"

We never get phone numbers; never a need. Felix just put on a wry smile and handed me the pad. I waited until I thought she might be home and I called her up as the concerned civil servant that I was. She readily agreed to let me re-examine those bruised ribs and I spent the rest of the summer learning about the truly uninhibited.

The Rambler should never have been on the road and Linda drove it like the hammers of hell. I had an out-patient appointment to have my lower wisdom teeth taken out at the Miriam Hospital and I needed a ride each way. Brian had an occasional gig chauffeuring a construction magnate so he brought me to the hospital in a Rolls Royce; certainly turned a few heads. He couldn't get back to pick me up so he called Linda and she must have enjoyed the fear on my largely helpless form. The nurse took me to the curb in a wheelchair like they still do and she and Linda pushed me into the car. "Now you're mine" she hissed as I buckled the lap belt and locked the door. We took off down I-95, weaving in and out at 80+ miles an hour and nary a cop when you need one, praying instead that the bald tires and the wandering front end would hold together one last time. We ended badly when a spat turned into a separation that brought a previous suitor back to Linda's interest.

Me and Steven kept the produce business until it didn't make sense any more. He was a good and loyal partner to have and he never offended anybody. Steven knew how much money we had at any given time just as I did and neither one of us ever bought so much as a pack of cigarettes with company funds. We made about $600 each for the entire summer and that included the $250 we got back from selling the truck. Dad thought we should have made about ten times that amount and didn't mind saying so and then he wondered out loud if perhaps there really was a whole lot more that Steven never saw. But Steven knew that Dad was just being Dad with nothing good to say, ever. I bought an Oldsmobile from Steven so that he could add the proceeds to his share of the business to buy a '67 Cougar. Then I bought a stereo to replace the one exWife had taken. In the end, I was relieved that Lakewood Hay&Grain was happy to have me back and KJ went to Chester Barrows Elementary School to begin the first grade of public education.

THE GREAT BLIZZARD

Cathy Quest was a couple of years older and she was once married to a guy who thought nothing of walking away. It left Cathy in a bit of a tizzy over whether or not she should invest that much of herself in anybody ever again. Still, she was game to try and she trusted me enough that we could be secure in each other's company. Love might have happened had she dropped her guard a little, but in the end she sought comfort only in herself.

The State of Rhode Island and Providence Plantations was handed a glimpse of colonial heritage when the Blizzard of '78 descended upon the land. It was such a sensation that there's even a picture book in hardcover. Everything came to a standstill as government reacted with almost no planning and even less available funding for such a profound emergency. The weather service had forecast a true nor'easter but those usually arrive warm and wet as they race up the coast. This one came in plenty wet but it ran into a cold front and stalled over southern New England; the severity was upon us without much notice. Rhode Island was paralyzed far longer than Massachusetts or Connecticut but thankfully, there was no more than the usual calamity and nothing burned.

I was at the lumberyard when the storm arrived early and it started snowing really hard right away. I left at noon, loaded up at the Star Market across the street, and chained up the Pontiac I had bought from Mr. Fontaine. I grabbed up KJ and drove to Roger Williams Hospital to pick up Cathy Quest because she was afraid to drive in the deep snow and didn't think she could make it all the way home. We got off the highway and on to Elmwood Avenue, where cars were already sliding to a permanent stop. Cathy was happy enough to stay at our house; she had even thought to pack a bag that morning in case she got stuck at the hospital.

It was beautiful, how it snowed. Everything covered in white, over and over again. When it stopped, there was 30" down in most places and every move in every direction had to be thought out. It wasn't hard – no one was going anywhere in a hurry.

The fire department called that night since guys from out of town couldn't get in or said they couldn't. I spent a number of days in a row on Rescue 2 while Cathy stayed with KJ. I was my own relief day and night until finally the snow was cleared and life returned to normal.

KJ and all his little friends had a great time; Cathy Quest did not. This would be KJ's first extended stay with a woman who was not his mother or his grandmother. Cathy Quest had never had children of her own and no real experience in living among them as an adult. Now she was thrust into a custodial situation with a six year old child whom she really only knew in passing. We had once briefly discussed an eventual live - in situation but there were a lot of "ifs" and no real plan and nothing KJ was aware of. Still, KJ opted for killing this baby in its crib - the very thought of living other than how we had up until now. He tramped snow through the kitchen from the back door and after Cathy mopped it up, he tramped in through the front. Then he brought Rusty through and added some friends. A few days into this, they let me off for an overnight at home and all I wanted to do was lay down for a while.

"Not before you have a discussion with your son!!!"

Right after, I was passed out on the couch when Cathy woke me up because old Mrs. Anthony across the street was having congestive heart failure. I sat with her while we waited for rescue and an engine company and Captain Hanks who was the acting Deputy Chief showed up first. Mrs. Anthony went with Rescue and I went with Captain Hanks who had pressed me back into service for even more of a great time.

Cathy was a good fit for a long time. For my birthday, she assembled Mom and Dad for a very nice dinner at her apartment on a night that exWife had KJ. Mom wanted to meet this thoughtful gal who might love her son and Dad had to come so no one could say that he didn't do the least he could do. An amazing feat, that, getting Dad to go where he had no interest. You could always tell, because he wouldn't go on and on like he needed to make an impression. Dad just sat there and ate while Cathy and Mom made nice and I didn't spill anything. We ended because KJ and Jill Clayburg showed Cathy Quest that An Unmarried Woman could be just fine.

I had never made KJ a part of anyone I was dating other than Cathy and only then because of the snowstorm. KJ knew Liz and he had met redBeth but they meant almost nothing since they never threatened his mother's possible return. Earlier on after Wife left, KJ was very young and also very protective of his mother's image. Wife may have left, but she didn't leave *him* – not by any measure that he could accept. At every opportunity, KJ would choose to be with his mother - to comfort her perhaps, or to somehow declare and also to solicit an allegiance that had nothing or everything to do with me. It would be their solemn pact, that despite the custodial arrangement and the inconvenient displacement of exWife, life could be as normal as the absence of any significant others would allow.

We made the rounds every morning like we always had when we first discovered the "Doughnuttery" donut shop near Lakewood Hay&Grain. Ronny and Elaine who owned the place had no kids of their own and they loved it when me and KJ came in. There was an uncomfortable moment when someone asked about the absence of soon to be exWife but that happened about the same time somebody had carved off the end of Ronnie's nose so there was plenty to talk about. We'd go to Ted's New York System or the old Miami Diner that had the best coffee around and a waitress named Jeanne who was always really nice to us. She was blonde and older and she never got to know how much I really liked her, too. Ted was a great guy who was Greek and who had plenty of extended family that helped staff the place at one time or another. If you were a little short, you could run a tab with Ted that he'd keep in the cash register and never speak about. If you were really short, you could get a cash loan with a handshake, if he knew you.

All these places had their own cast of regular characters who came and went and who were good to me and KJ. We'd bop in on one or the other and then off to school and work in a cozy little world where everything was in its' place. But you could write TV scripts all day long about this poor little boy and his dad and none would even be close.

BC/AC

It had ended with redBeth before I spent the winter of '78 with Cathy Quest. I thought I was long over redBeth when she asked me to be "and guest" at Sophie's wedding. Sophie was an ER nurse who was always pleasant and much beloved in friendship and in marriage. In stark contrast stood redBeth who was having a very gray day in celebrating somebody else's happiness. She disappeared from our table so she could be with friends or perhaps that other guy I didn't know about. If I could have a do-over of Sophie's wedding, I would have caught a ride home with Carolyn. Carolyn had always turned my head but for reasons unknown, I had always thought that she was married or otherwise spoken for. We might have exchanged "hellos" in the ER but it would have been professional although I couldn't help but notice how attractive she would continue to become. Now we are face to face in the receiving line where I'm supposed to be with redBeth and Carolyn is alone with friends. We exchange pleasantries while I take in all she is before me and redBeth almost doesn't matter. Not long after, we meet again in the ER on a cold dreary day and I pass along something about how "Bermuda looks kind of nice about now..." and Carolyn agrees. "...and someone to go with" is left unsaid and suddenly we're a little awkward by ourselves.

Liz would always come by and we'd sit and talk and smoke and sometimes she'd even bring a load of laundry to run while we hung out. We'd commiserate about the attention and the accolades we thought we deserved from whom we thought we loved except now I wasn't any longer in love. So I had to ask:

"What about Carolyn Holland?"

Liz got right on board.

"She would be so perfect for you – has a little boy; very nice to be around. Can't say enough good – you should call her right up, right now. Go ahead. No Balls. $50 says..."

So of course she's in the phone book under C. Holland the way every other woman alone is listed and I call her up and I get her voice and a little apprehension in my own..

"You might not remember me but..."

Carolyn remembered me just fine and she agrees to a dinner date. I drove to Carolyn's apartment complex across the Providence River with written directions, the best of intentions, and the highest of hopes that the Olds wouldn't spit out its transmission tonight. The apartment is nice enough, exuding a degree of taste that the liberty bell lamps could never match. Not my idea of happily ever after, but secure enough to call home for anyone living almost alone. We take our leave and drive for half an hour to the Red Rooster Tavern where we feast on good fortune and forgettable fare, even though the food was great. We later part as we both know that we should, but next time she'd meet Rusty and it would seem like we had always been together.

In the beginning, both of our sons were largely indifferent to this hot new romance. Bobby had seen good men profess their love and loyalty before and KJ remained true to the value judgments that he had adopted from the time he was about four. Each of the other two parents took stock of the developing situation and redoubled efforts to make their own presence known. KJ became even more drawn to his mother and more withdrawn from me, like he needed to choose. Bobby found some new faith in his own father who was once again paying attention but not his child support.

We began in October and we were arm in arm by November and Gram would decidedly announce us to the entire family at Gramp's Christmas Eve festivity. Then she grilled Carolyn about everything she could ever want to know about her second grandson's bride to be. Gram was first, last, and always a mother and she was highly judgmental of women who made other choices and of those who worked away from the home. She had some difficulty with the fact that not everybody would remain a home maker the way she had but she also had Gramp who had always made her comfort possible. Carolyn could certainly hold her own about making her way in this world and it would have been amusing to watch a modern woman engage a Victorian intellect except that Gram was always so serious. We learned long ago that if you just tell Gram what she wants to hear, she'll give you a candy bar but Carolyn didn't know that.

There was only one misgiving that threatened our new life together. Carolyn called me at the station – all kinds of distraught – about how we were too far too fast and how she couldn't suffer another crushing regret if I were not the real deal and then there were the kids and ....

"Talk to Liz; call her up – right now."

"No, no, you don't understand..."

"No, I don't – but I'm captive here; I can't leave, can't come to see you - call Liz – she knows better than anybody!."

So Carolyn calls Liz who vouches for everything she knows about me or has ever heard me say or has ever seen when she's been around me and KJ and she makes it O.K. Me and Carolyn re-wrap the package and seal it as tightly as two people have ever been.

Carolyn is descended from the Bonniol family elders who

emigrated from Saint Quentin, a city in the north of France on the River Somme. They were jewelers who fit right in as part of a predominant industry in Rhode Island. The elder family shared a small house near the Providence/Cranston line and they worked in a little shop out back that later became a garden shed. The offspring learned early on that small time manufacturing was no way to fend off abject poverty and after WW II, they all went on to do something else. Now all that remains of the company is the safe, which we've held onto since the sons of the elders passed on.

Carolyn is the second daughter of Louis and Emily Bonniol who once lived in Barrington among the very well to do. She grew up Catholic although not nearly as smitten and got into more mischief through high school than I ever would have dared. Carolyn was no exception to the rebellious nature of our time and she found herself with child just as I had. She married with some apprehension to a guy who would also defy monogamy and Carolyn soon found herself an unmarried head of household. That guy went on to marry another good woman with whom he would have two more children and he eventually left them in a similar situation. Carolyn's mom and dad would never turn their back on their struggling daughter because that's not who they were as parents or as a family. Even as she began to rebuild her life, Carolyn never saw herself as helpless and she never counted herself as down or out. Before and during our life together, Carolyn always stood for herself and for others - sometimes at great expense and diminution.

Carolyn's dad spent all of WW II aboard a couple of PT boats, one of which got blown out of the water. He'd had a number of close calls with annihilation in the Pacific theatre, but worse by far was the early debilitating heart attack that his daughter the brand new ER nurse had to helplessly endure. It was a beauty and it was before the advent of by-pass and stents and you either got through it medically or you didn't. Louie did O.K. – lived to be almost 80 – but a number of other health issues would hinder the man who mostly worried about everybody else. The missus was a little less selfless. As the mom, Emily would turn out to be more pragmatic, a little less patient, and somewhat insensitive. But I loved their daughter and I was Jack Caito's grandson and that was all they needed to hear. When I told Gramp who I was serious about, he went on to explain what good friends he and Louie were. They went way back to when Louie and his brother first founded Superior Sheet Metal, a company that furnished the HVAC ductwork for the homes that Gramp built.

The new in-laws would engage the very high brow Squantum Club for the first formal wedding of their second daughter and wouldn't have it any other way. There was room for only so many guests and we took the view that we would invite the people who were close to us while we chose to overlook family that didn't matter. The family that didn't matter didn't care, but a couple of people who claimed friendship to us were a little offended at being omitted. We fell into some of the usual potholes and also a few craters that come with planning a wedding and new mother in law poisoned us the night before with some bad crab. Everybody was able to keep their own comfort and as soon as we could get clean away, me and Carolyn were jetting to London.

Confounding all of this just a little was another estrangement with Dad over some loss of control that was deemed to be all my fault. David had a Honda 500 that one of the twin brothers would buy so that David could buy a 750. Twin brother had asked Dad for a short loan and of course Dad said no so the rest of us helped out, me least of all. Dad went ballistic - said that if he wanted twin brother to have that bike, he would have given him the money and who the hell were we (me) to usurp his authority.

"AND TELL THAT LITTLE S.O.B. TO STAY
ON HIS OWN SIDE OF TOWN!!!"

We blew it off because everybody is over 18 and to hell with

Dad who was only about not lending the cash. Later on, it comes to David's attention that twin brother is up to his eyeballs with addiction to any and all of whatever he could get himself into; gets good and accelerated in his head and also on the bike. David kidnaps the bike so that twin brother doesn't kill himself and stashes it at my house until we can think of what to do next. Once again, clueless Dad gets on his own side and calls up to say he'll either call the cops or come across town to "...spread some flesh" to which I reply, "Still don't get it, do you?" Big ones, me, and Dad just steps right over that to make a few more threats.

The wedding is only a few weeks away and the invitations had long ago been sent out. We don't really know what Mom and Dad will do but in the end, Mom makes it clear to Dad that they'll be coming. Nobody wants to have to explain this all once again to Gram and Gramp and besides, David's wedding to Suzi is coming up right after. Mom won't be denied and Dad's just going to have to make nice enough and forget about the bunch in his shorts that we *all* had a hand in making. Gram and Gramp got to know full well what it's been like over the years between me and Dad but no one can explain it. How much they ever knew about some of Dad's darker secrets would be anybody's guess and I expect that Dad didn't give a whit what anybody thought. Gramp always clung to the Fifth Commandment because he could never be anything but an honorable father and he could never quite accept that his only daughter was married to the ogre that I made Dad out to be. But I was the affable grandson who always came around and Dad was always the guy who hated everything he laid his eyes upon. Everybody saw that part.

Some time after the wedding, I found myself turning into their driveway because once again, the peace is apparently mine to make. Face to face with Mom alone, I can scarcely recognize the broken, withered woman she has become. She is 50 - looks older than Gram who is almost 80. She lives on bad coffee, bad memories and Winston 100's and she prays for a peaceful death, sooner rather than later. Mom has paid dearly for her allegiance to a man who has cost her the love and companionship of children and grandchildren alike. At the conclusion of my very last words with Mom I ask why in the end, she remains. She replies:

"What would you have me do?"

Mom insisted that if I cannot accept my father in the very same way that I would seek to favor her, then I would have neither. Dad would expect nothing less than this valiant stand that Mom chose on their behalf. She added that it would be unacceptable for us to see her alone.

There is no way to explain to an eight year old boy any of the preceding or the reasoning behind it since I have no clear understanding of it myself. All of the mystery of how we got from there to here can only be summed up by the admission that we are unlike any other family I grew up knowing. Threats were kept while promises were not and Dad did exactly as he pleased with no regard for others whatsoever. It probably wasn't fair to my son or to Mom that suddenly we weren't seeing her over grievances having only to do with me, but KJ seemed largely unfazed and Dad suffered no loss at all. I resolved forever that my son would see no more of this and that I would never be the man that my father was.

Me and Carolyn had chosen the White Church in Barrington for its beauty and splendor and for the minister who also shared pastoral duties at Rhode Island Hospital. It was a Congregational Church – United Church of Christ – and there's a story about how in colonial times, oxen dragged the church across the frozen Barrington River. Rev. O'Brien was accommodating enough but he insisted upon some pre-marital inquisition, sort of like the Catholics. But unlike the Catholics who are more concerned with the preservation of the institution of the church, Rev. O'Brien seemed more interested in parts of our being that we may not have explored so well. Could we believe that our respective offspring would enjoy this new life as much as we would? We had no reason to think otherwise. Could our children accept that there would be someone other than their own selves to consider? Of course - why on earth not? We'd had lengthy discussions about what it could all be like. Did Carolyn and I accept that circumstances far beyond our control would become the avalanche of hurt feelings and unintended consequences that no one could ever imagine? Actually, that's what the Rev. O'Brien didn't ask... that last one.

We did not seek outright permission from our children to plan a future together although our sons were certainly offered plenty of opportunity to speak up about individual concerns. They had both been invited to participate as ring bearers for the ceremony and we carefully watched their behavior as the date grew closer. For Bobby, it appeared to be all good - that he could only gain from a situation where a real dad would offer time and attention and ask nothing in return. For KJ, any situation that didn't offend or threaten his mother might be O.K. He would sometimes engage and he would sometimes withdraw but he appeared to have found the situation to be mostly tolerable because Carolyn mostly never imposed. As Bobby and KJ spent more and more time together, a competition developed for whatever attention they both wanted at the same time. The older boy tried to elbow his way in while my son did his best to hold everybody off so that he could continue to be his mother's champion.

Shortly before the wedding, my own commitment came up against a triumvirate of temptation. BellaDonna was without a lover and called to see if I wanted to play. I had all but forgotten her and now I suspect she was ready to settle down or perhaps just settle. It was nice to hear from her, but there was closure in our last goodbye and there would be no regret.

Cathy Quest called to ask about my well being but she had made such a point of remaining an unmarried woman that I couldn't readily imagine that she had reconsidered. We hadn't kept in touch; never saw each other again after we had ended although we hadn't ended badly at all. Didn't matter. I was happy to tell her that I'd be married in a couple of weeks.

Vanity appeared in the person of redBeth with no warning at all, but I expected her all along. The ER was abuzz about the hot new romance and ever since Sophie's wedding, there was hope for a happily ever after for me and Carolyn from a number of people. RedBeth had been with someone from the ER off and on during our time together but she offered her heart to neither. He knew about me but I didn't know about him until much later. Carolyn says that in the end, I simply didn't matter. But here she was, standing in my kitchen and purring just a little, looking to re-claim what had always been justly hers. In return she would get as little as she ever wanted and more than she deserved. I kissed her goodbye the way I would have kissed Gram and sent redBeth on her way forever.

Me and David moved everything out of the East Providence apartment to Piedmont St. on a single Saturday. There was an anxious moment over a heavy convertible sofa that we intended to throw over the balcony so it could land in a million pieces but Carolyn returned with the pizza sooner than expected and caught us red-handed. Then the damn thing opened up in the middle of the stairwell to a number of very bad words. At Piedmont St. the very first to go was the old mattress on the floor followed shortly by the liberty bell lamps. There was some discussion about the multi-floral wallpaper of our bedroom but it was nearly new and there were other priorities.

At the house on Piedmont St. the boys each had their very own bedrooms; KJ's wallpapered with jet airplanes and Bobby's done in "Star Wars". All of the bedrooms were tiny and we shared the only bathroom which was upstairs and there was no practical space in the house for another. After exWife and the Twogae had made a mess of pretending to remodel, I had overhauled the bathroom with an Owens-Corning two piece fiberglass tub and shower unit and I put down some cheap vinyl floor over the plywood. Shortly after we became me and Carolyn, I gutted the entire bathroom and started over with real ceramic tile that I learned to do for myself before there was Home Depot. Jay Castergine's dad got me started because he was the best tile guy I knew; a friend of Gramp's, and a friend to me.

Right after the wedding, there were baseball try-outs where parents got to hope that their kid wouldn't be among the last to be chosen. Our new coach would be Jim Haworth who was a schoolteacher who knew everything the Red Sox ever did. The assistant was Rod Bouressa and we all got to be good friends along with a number of other parents who got involved. This was an instructional league where basic skills were taught and where both of our boys belonged since KJ was so much younger and Bobby had never played. Jim was a terrific head coach who cared more about personal development and having fun than he did about the happenstance of winning. Most runs were walked in because almost nobody could pitch, the notable exception being one of the Foster brothers who could strike out most adults. We were especially proud of Jill Sullivan, who could field at least as well as any of the boys and she could hit better than most. The only real distraction was when exWife took up with another kid's dad.

Life settled down to where I could leave Lakewood Hay&Grain behind forever and Carolyn cut her time in the ER almost in half and we got to extend the honeymoon a little. My wedding gift from Carolyn was a little plywood runabout that we hooked up to the Dodge and launched in the bay to fish for flounder and tautog. We'd follow the tide to get the boat back in so that Carolyn could get to work on time. In the summer we loaded up the truck with kids and Rusty and drove up to what we called "the trench" in Hope - a village in Scituate that harkens back to colonial times. The trench was actually the sluiceway to the old gatehouse that moved water through the Valley Lace Company back in the 1800's when textile reigned in Rhode Island. It was a straight shot of crystal clear water about ten feet deep, contained by giant slabs of granite and a lifetime of happy memories. One time, Rusty and a Doberman got into a shouting match across the trench from each other and then the dobie jumped in. Swimming for a dobie is the act of staying alive whereas Golden Retrievers chug along like a 'gator. Rusty swam right over the dobie and held him under until the kid that owned the dobie had to dive in to save his dog. It was hilarious.

That first summer that we all lived on Piedmont St., everybody got a first hand look at just what happens when you hear all those sirens. Carolyn was in the kitchen when the kids came in:

"What are you guys doing?"

"Watching Eric's house on fire!"

Carolyn looked outside and sure enough, she saw what we saw as we pulled up - smoke and flame roaring out the second floor window. Me and Louie Pelico donned Scotts and the Engine crew did not and soon they were overcome inside the house and had to get out. Louie and I took an inch and a half up the stairs on fog pattern and blew that fire out in about 30 seconds, but what Carolyn and the kids saw was us dashing in and not coming right out. A fire of highly suspicious origin and perhaps born of little fingers, it would have made great TV but it rocked Carolyn a little.

We were well known to our immediate neighbors as they were to us and it was almost all good. Rusty and the Boxer two doors down would fight to the death if they could but all of the people got along fine. We took everybody's kids swimming, conditions being that the parents had to know where they were and if you said you could swim, you'd better not be lying. As neighborhoods turn over, almost everybody we left years ago is still there except for some husbands. Four died, three became estranged, and one sleeps in his '63 Beetle on the front lawn. Just before we moved to the house around the corner, Me and David and Suzi were waiting for Carolyn to get out of the shower when there was a terrible commotion at the back door.

"Gerry, Gerry, My mother!! my mother !!..."

One of the twin daughters was in a panic, terror stricken at watching Rita collapse. I jumped the back fence and rushed in to find Rita on the floor and unconscious and she deteriorates right into cardiac arrest. Rescue is still minutes away but David tosses Carolyn and my off duty medical bag over the fence. I hadn't thought about who was on but when Hawk and JB walked in, we couldn't have been any better off. Carolyn directed the code 99* and she got us an I.V. and everything went about as slick as it could have; the ER couldn't have gotten it any better. All the way to the hospital we pushed on Rita but she had suffered the infarct that the old people pray for - except she wasn't old.

Right after that tragic episode, we moved to a house right around the corner on Park View Blvd. that I had always had my eye on - a beautiful cape on a double corner lot. We wanted more room but we didn't want to displace the kids to another neighborhood or a new school. A nice lady who lived alone owned the house and it was slowly deteriorating beyond what she could manage and she finally accepted that she should give it up. The first day the "For Sale" sign was up, I put an offer on the house that was readily accepted. The house was bigger in every way than the house on Piedmont St. but the boys would have to share a bedroom for a while. We would draw plans and begin construction of a two floor addition that would double the size of the kitchen and add a laundry and another bedroom. I would pay the boys to help until they wouldn't so I hired one of their friends to back fill the foundation. They complained bitterly to Carolyn that since I wouldn't pay them to leave the work undone, then they would just go to work for the kid that I did hire. They'd show me...

The house didn't have a dishwasher so we thought that it might be a good experience to have the kids wash and dry dishes - sort of establish a few chores like our parents did with us. They were about 9 and 12 respectively - old enough to learn to be of service. But they decidedly weren't having any of this and Carolyn wasn't satisfied with how the dishes were done or that the kitchen sink was forever full. So we got a Kitchenaid dishwasher like we had on Piedmont St. and soon enough, the kitchen sink remained full once again. We had a beautiful lawn that no one would help cut and we put in a swimming pool that no one would help to clean. When their laundry was neatly stacked at the foot of the bed, the boys would simply dump it back into the clothes hamper rather than put it away. They were beyond untidy and wouldn't pick up a thing and sometimes I had to go upstairs with a rake. But all the while we were expected to meet every conceivable wish and listen to all their crap because they perceived themselves as neglected children of divorce and deserved every consideration. In Dad's house, they would have been picking up their teeth.

We started to go off the rails about the time Carolyn returned to Rhode Island College for her Baccalaureate in Nursing. She had initially trained at the original Rhode Island Hospital School of Nursing which was very strict and regimented with housemothers and such. Carolyn had always been such a promising student that even when she got to be with child, the school found a way to keep her. I was happy enough to support Carolyn's ambition to achieve; I thought we all would. The BSN would lead to a career path in management and a future that would benefit the kids most of all. The children however, were caught up in their own struggle to out do each other in the realm of the selfish. They fought, they sulked, and they tried to hold us hostage to what they thought they could always require of the other parent. This worked out for KJ a whole lot better than it did for Bobby since exWife would turn herself inside out to comply. It only added to the animosity between the boys. It got worse when exWife got married once again, just so she could be married. Her words – not mine.

Bobby didn't exactly share his mother's thirst for knowledge and he didn't care for schoolwork, or any work at all. Carolyn was still part time on an evening shift in the ER and she could schedule herself around my time at the station. But evening hours would be for me to regulate and there would be no TV or video games until homework was done. Bobby's answer to that was to simply bring home no assignments so he could do almost nothing, at least until report cards were presented. My response was that he could just sit on the end of his bed for all I cared - there would still be no TV. But where I said "no" Carolyn would say "yes" and there was no wherewithal to govern anyone's behavior.

We almost didn't make it together, I of the most impertinent temperament and she the most forgiving. It was always about the kids who expected everything they could imagine from us and then some. Carolyn would fret at Christmastime about whether there was enough while I remember wishing that I was one of our kids. Of the children who would never remember her birthday or reach out on Mother's Day, Carolyn would just brush it off. I would not. For me, the disregard that our two angels maintained for anyone other than themselves got to be more than outrageous. Soon enough, it was me who was the issue, mostly because of everything that had drawn me to love Carolyn and the happiness we would share with our children. How on earth could our children so disagree?

Judgmental Bastards

Google "Larrivee" and it will usually take you to the guitar makers of world renown. We ain't them. We're the ones who could just as easily have been the Hatfields or the McCoys but the war would have always been familial with a number of other adversaries on the side. We can feud on any number of fronts at one time and seem almost invisible doing it - right up until the hammer comes down. I've been hammered and I've hammered a few right back and so have all of us at one time or another. We don't ambush anybody or set anyone up for failure, and karma doesn't always reward the good that we do in ways we can appreciate. We welcome whatever works well for us but we don't always learn from our mistakes. There can be anger management issues. Most people won't put up with very much of how we learned to be from Dad and even though Dad's was an extreme case of intolerance, he had to get it from somewhere. We used to think that it was from Dad having no father and from having so little as a youngster but his best pal Mud Duck was no better off and he was a fine dad to all of his daughters and he and his wife were good to us as well.

We don't care much about who hates us because it would never be anybody that we had any real need of knowing in the first place. Its' an attitude that was handed down through Dad who got it from his mother's side that goes all the way back over a hundred years to when somebody abandoned three adorable little girls. One of those little girls was Dad's mom who died when I was about two – thoroughly beaten down by life. There is a thread of familial disconnect throughout our history. Me and Jazzy share a presumption of acceptance into anybody's company - at least until they demonstrate otherwise - and we are both overwhelmingly stung by rejection. I'll usually just take the walk; never stay where I'm not welcome. I've always been able to distinguish a true adversary from a run of the mill pain in the ass, but Dad treated them all the same. Towards his end, Dad was even growling at his closest friends. Within our family, all of Mom and Dad's kids barely speak and all of our own kids wouldn't even recognize each other. Growing up, we never had much to do with any of our other cousins. It is an unseemly culture that we've developed, that our young seem to grow up and leave us behind - the rear view fading as though it all never happened. Dad could have taken this in a different direction but he kept to his other life instead. Mom was so defeated that she needed a savior of her own. Other families seem to live within each other's lives and to care about what happens to the children, even after they're grown. There was love in Carolyn's family that was palpable and Gramp would always say that he loved his children and his grandchildren "...not one more than the other" while Gram always worried that we'd put out an eye. It's not like we've had no living examples.

Your time is now; so wrote John Mellancamp. There may be eternal salvation for the faithful few who chose the right god, but the rest of us will be dust or maybe a rabbit or a butterfly or a ghost if we're lucky. From the beginning of my time with Carolyn, I have lived in the moment with her while we drew up a halo protecting the sanctity of our love. My son would never appreciate this and he seemed to take it all rather personally that he himself alone would not always be first and foremost to my attention. I failed to address this because I always took for granted the longer view that I had reserve enough for everybody and that KJ would always know the son that he was to me. But he would never put aside his resentment, even when I no longer hated his mother. I would not reveal her trespasses and KJ would be spared the details of the loss that he still needed to hold me responsible for. Carolyn realized all of this right from the very beginning. She tried to be a peacemaker and got badly bitten for her efforts. Nevertheless, she was a guardian of KJ's safety and wellbeing and later on, an advocate for his future.

One of my son's more critical observations would be that of the Larrivee obsession with a dollar or more. Born of never having quite enough, the shortsighted conclusion would be that having money is more important to us than anything it could buy. Quite the contrary; money is simply a means of exchange - an identification of value, sometimes even of each other. We Larrivees work hard to turn a buck - usually at something arduous- and then try to put a few more together for something worthwhile. What complicates the issue is how long and how hard and at what cost do we have to expend ourselves to cover everybody's needs. Kids need shoes; kids want Nike. Kid wants a bike; has to be a Univega. The Visa bill starts to crawl across the table and still, the kids don't understand why they can't have everything they ever thought of. Growing up, we learned for ourselves that our wants were many, our needs were few, and that we'd have to fulfill a few of our own expectations. Mom would say "...and people in hell want ice water..."

There's always a way to have enough. Create more, reduce need, eliminate waste and teach the children to do the same. Save for a rainy day and tighten your belt a notch or two where you need to. When cash is a little tight, you don't buy artwork. Our kids grew up believing they were entitled to burn through every dollar they could get and what we wouldn't give them, they stole from us. The incentive for us to be good and caring began to dissipate - more for me than for Carolyn - and the two little boys who had been the joy of our singular lives joined forces to create a storm centered right over our house. As the wind and the rain and the tide grew to hurricane force, we hunkered down to ride it out. We declared to both that they would not be with us forever; we circled our wagon and crawled inside.

There got to be no way around needing another part time job. Carolyn was straight out between work and school and we were adding on to the house so that our progeny could have separate bedrooms. I hired on to drive a dump truck and run other heavy equipment for a guy who owned a local nursery and garden center. It would have been a great job if all I had to do was run the equipment but if there were no delivery orders, all I could do was stay and work in the field or not work at all. The money was pretty good and soon we couldn't do without it but I knew my back would never hold out digging two hundred pound tree balls by hand. I hooked up with a couple of friends who did roofing and re-models which was only a little less demanding. I doubled up on the physical therapy routine and took Feldene and other stuff to make the back problem go away.

Carolyn left the ER to work upstairs in surgical intensive care. There would be more opportunity and different politics and eventually she would become an assistant nurse manager. We knew that teenage drivers and college expenses would soon be upon us and in fact, some already were. Carolyn took another breath and plowed on to earn a Master of Science in Nursing at URI after graduating magna cum laude from Rhode Island College. Our lives got a little bigger and the family got to ski in Europe and our kids got almost everything they wanted. That got a little lopsided on KJ's behalf because exWife was now happy to provide what we wouldn't. Bobby's father made a splash here and there when he thought he needed to but that stopped once the family court required more of him. We banked every child support dollar we ever got for Bobby's college future with no idea of what that might be.

I got promoted to Rescue Lieutenant about the same time that Dad the big shot Teamster lost his job thanks to Jimmy Carter and the congress. We had grown up listening to Dad sermonize about the all - powerful union that would dare to even challenge President Kennedy. When trucking got deregulated and the National Freight Contract became irrelevant, so did a number of union outfits. Johnson Motor Lines promptly closed up operations and sold their trucks and Mr. Number Two in the whole barn was reduced to working out of the union hall on a per diem basis. We were still on the outside so we weren't around for the fallout which by all accounts wasn't pretty. Dad the big shot Teamster never forgave the company or the union for letting this happen and then he became a Republican. He got clobbered running for a seat on the city council that the other guy had already sewn up. Our firefighter's union made a point of telling me that they weren't going to support Dad because they had always been for the other guy and besides, Dad had said out loud that he'd move to take the beds out of the fire stations. As a consolation prize, they put Dad in charge of Animal Control. One of Dad's official duties was to round up Rusty who had always had the run of the neighborhood. He brought Rusty home to Carolyn and related in a most professional manner that dogs must be restrained from roaming at will. Rusty lost his job as everybody's dog but he was older now and it was probably long overdue. I took it kind of personal just the same - one more reason to hate the meanest guy I ever knew, now that he was the dog catcher.

And No Religion, Too

I was able to bring our kids to the brink of religion but so far, no one has taken any kind of a leap that I am aware of. Quite the opposite, actually. To my mind the concept of a deity should exist more in line with what we *should* be doing for ourselves and for each other, if we were truly created in the image of the God that the bible thumpers think they know. And most of those people are pretty fat and happy with a lot they should be way more thankful for, living rather large as it were. Ideally, the world would be engaged in the purest form of socialism, living in perfect harmony where everyone would be satisfied with what they had earned, over and above an established threshold where nobody went hungry. Add a little grace and it becomes the heaven we've all been told about except that we're not made that way. Instead, we'd all be bored stiff and wanting. John Lennon - who came to us only in peace - might have enjoyed it, but he could also spend a week in bed. The rest of us are more like manic honeybees just trying to keep everybody fed. Some lead, some follow, and some would grab up everything they could for themselves because capitalism says they can. So it's the living, breathing humanity in this particular genre that you might consider to be the fly in God's ointment and it surely is a carnival. But so what?

What would Jesus do? No, Seriously. Even if Jesus Christ is not your true god or savior or commander, what did he ever take the wrong view of? Or a kind and loving god by any other name and in any other language or any other color - they would all be pals enough to label as one and the same in spirit. How many crusades have the deities ordered or authorized, and in who's name or interest? War in the name of Jesus Christ actually begat more of Christendom and created the societies that have evolved ever since to fight the heathens. But who thinks that Jesus Christ or anybody who spoke for Jesus Christ first hand would invite it? Since no one ever told Christians that being fed to the lions was a good thing, at some point they were destined to abandon that form of sanctimony and rally against their oppressors. Like anyone else with nothing to lose, they fought hard and they fought well and then they took their show on the road. Anybody with enough ambition and charisma could raise an army in God's name and that army would follow him anywhere until the food ran out or they got annihilated.

There have been a lot of those people, people who are themselves convinced and would have you believe that they were spoken to by God. Or that they were close to someone who had been spoken to by God. Or they were descended from people who knew all about this but couldn't quite place the why in it. My personal favorite was Marshall Applewhite, the guy who founded Heaven's Gate in DelMar, California. He got all of those people to join him in death to await the arrival of the alien spacecraft that was following the sodium trail of the Hale-Bop Comet. Apparently the sodium trail had been observed in other comets but not from the tail. Applewhite took this as a sign from God to off his gang so they could all be whisked away to Paradise.

The sad side is that the charlatans among us aren't all that apparent and you have to choose carefully about what to teach your children. The short answer is that there is a galaxy of gray between sin and absolution and we compromise and justify and quantify what we do in between. But an actual God the Father keeping numbers on all of us? I honestly don't see how anybody could know for sure. Does George Carlin rot in hell for consolidating the Ten Commandments? Does Gerry Fallwell now reside next door to Jesus, or maybe just down the street? In my early Catholic world the wages of sin would start with a little heat in Purgatory just for failing to pay attention during catechism. To my knowledge, there isn't just a good talking to if you weren't too bad - only suffering - and plenty to go around at that. If you were unfortunate enough to get cancelled with a mortal sin on your head, you were destined to a pretty tough eternity. The devil had to eat too, at least in Sister Helena's world. She used to tell me and everyone around me that I was the devil's own child; that she could see the devil's tail raveled around my legs. It put the fear of eternal damnation front and center to my first grade self and I got to fear God as well as Dad. But the anonymity of the confessional at least meant that you could say some stuff out loud that Dad would never hear and then do a penance to get God past it. I never confessed anything, ever, to Dad nor did I ever tell a priest the whole truth, either. I might already be a goner.

I never felt that there should be no religious tolerance so I began taking the kids to the Edgewood Congregational Church where they could attend church classes while the service went on. It was entirely my choice since the Congregational Church (United Church of Christ) had made a forgiving enough impression to enlist my interest and Carolyn said it was O.K. We would never return to Catholicism; shame on that bunch for what they did to all those kids. Another hand of God that went awry for sure, but Catholics won't dare to disbelieve enough to fix what's wrong. They would rather have you believe that theirs is the best club to join because they had it all figured out. Back in the olden times, though, I bet there were a few questions after the Saracens kicked their asses.

I would have traded places with the kids in a heartbeat just to get out from under the Reverend who prattled on about nothing of inspiration or interest. He was a big scary looking guy who could have raised the roof against sin but instead, he'd have you asleep in minutes. The kids were taught by some of the church elders who sincerely believed that they were serving a greater good in passing on their version of what God wants. My son got a much greater helping of theology later on that also failed to include the Fifth Commandment. Where we sent my son to high school, theology is required study. He didn't care to speak about it and I just figured he was blowing off more of it than I ever dared to. Bobby had some Catholic background also but it wasn't on TV so it didn't stay with him for long. In the end, our attendance at the Edgewood Congregational Church lacked any inspiration whatsoever. When the kids didn't want to go any more, nobody did.

I have known a fair number of Catholic priests in my time, some who stand accused but most who are not, never have been, never will be. Shame on all the others for how they would stand for God. No one ever hit on me. I don't know if that was just my good fortune or I never appeared vulnerable or maybe I just wasn't all that attractive. Or they knew about Dad. But some of the fathers were funny as hell in light of what they had to swear off in order to be a priest. Father Flanagan read my report card to me as they did back then and sometimes he'd nod off in mid-sentence. You'd sit next to him at Sister's desk while he groused at you about what he considered a deficiency and suddenly there was silence. Then Sister would hurry to his side and you'd be on your way back to your seat so the next kid could have fun. It took all day with red-eyed Father Flanagan but Monsignor Drury would get through it in an hour. He needed to since he didn't have a whole lot of time left. What had started out as a blemish on Monsignor's lip turned into a hideous experience that left him minus a lot of his mouth. We prayed for him daily but he died just the same.

Another of the Fathers was a handsome young priest with a military cut who was a favorite of the Twogae. They even got to call him "Ned". He did not remain a priest nor did many of the other young celibates who followed him right out the door. One of them married a Margaret who might have been one of the O'Houlihan sisters. They were very much in love at the time but imagine the hell you must get for seducing a priest. Budlong's fantasy was to get over on a nun but I never imagined that to be any fun because I never thought of nuns as women or even female. They were just another agent of fear in an endless parade of scary adults beginning with Dad. Sister said this and Father means that and fasting and sacrifice and no opening Christmas presents until after Mass. Boy, did they ever hate Santa Claus! And TV. It used to be that we all went to 8 o'clock Mass with Gram and Gramp because Dad didn't go and Mom didn't drive and we damn well had to be ready when Gramp pulled into the driveway. Not a lot was said about the missing head of his own household not being in church, but I'd bet a lot of guys wished they could be so lucky, me included.

Catholic education was a unique blend of fear, intimidation, corporal punishment, and a dash of hope. Everything was learned through recitation and repetition - so much so that you would do it in your sleep, wake up to it, and carry it around all day. You could pick this right out of when the Mass was on TV. The incantations in monotone made it sound so much like a pagan ritual that you would think that you were watching an old black and white Tarzan movie. We learned it by chanting along with Sister; no idea what we were saying. The Latin Mass was even worse and the people pretending to pay attention never really knew what was being said, either. Kind of made you look forward to the hymns that nobody sang, but they had a pretty good organist. A choir might have been nice, but most Catholics aren't happy enough to sing so they'd have had to hire one. Maybe they should assign singing as penance - then you'd know who had pled guilty and who was sitting in silent sin. I was so bored with it all that if I couldn't conjure up a decent daydream, I'd practice holding my breath. I never really knew for how long until the year Gram and Gramp got us wrist watches for Christmas. Then Vatican II dumped the Latin Mass so that the priest could interact more with the congregation in English. That mattered so much that I learned to hold my breath for two full minutes.

There were two churches side by each – St Mary's and St. Ann's. They shared a parking lot and staggered Mass enough so that all the good Catholics coming to Mass wouldn't be cussing out those who were trying to leave, it being The Lord's Day and all. It happened a lot anyway and Gramp would avoid it by parking in the cemetery. Once we parked on the rectory side of St Ann's but as we walked in from that direction in front of the bell tower, a pigeon in the belfry crapped on Gramp's shoulder. It was pretty funny to hear a "goddamit" on the way in to church and we went back to parking on the cemetery side. Gramp always brought a bar of hard paraffin wax to church because one of the front doors always stuck a little in the jamb. Later on, Monsignor corralled him into fixing that door the way Gramp said it should have been done in the first place.

At St. Ann's there was always something in stained glass or the Gospels to conjure up a daydream in any little boy who could imagine living in the time of Christ with horses instead of camels. Later on Loretta Dybala and her family would file past our pew as they headed for the front lines. Loretta was pretty and blonde and older and she might have gone to a private school because we never saw her anywhere else. But she sure was something to look at and I'm glad they sat in front of us because I'd have been caught staring for sure. The mom was just as beautiful and you could tell old Ed was way wicked proud of his family, especially when his son showed up in formal military attire. Ed and Gramp were friendly, but not pals.

Ida May Markey always wore a new hat. I swear I never saw the same one on her twice. She was a looker in a world where everybody else's mom was just a mom and it got me to noticing older women. By then I was going to church almost exclusively with Gram and Gramp because now that Mom could drive, she chose to go to the 9:15 or even the 10:30. That would burn up most of Sunday morning and when Mom opted for a later Mass, Gramp went right to the 7 because he didn't like blowing most of a day, either. I just had to be sitting on the breezeway when he was ready to leave and stay out of the way when he backed the Caddy out. The best part for a kid like me was the ride home.

We'd stop to get Italian bread at Garzilli's for Sunday dinner and I'd eat the heel off of it while I waited for Gram to wind up Gramp. It was never long in coming either because if there was anything that could piss Gramp off, it was Gram. She lectured about every imaginable impropriety and poor Gramp had to live with her. We'd leave Garzilli's in Knightsville, start down Phenix Avenue past old lady Soprano's vegetable stand and by the time we got to the bottom of the long hill that was Scituate Avenue, she'd have him in blisters. That first Caddy had a 472 that was all stroke and as the volume got turned up, so did the land speed. One time Gramp was headed past 80 which is really fast for old people but not for that Caddy.

JACK!!! THE CHILD!! WE HAVE THE CHILD!!!

He just looked over at her and then he let off it a little. When she didn't say anything more, he let off of it altogether. A couple more rides like that, and Gram shut up most of the time but no one was any happier for it.

The other church was St. Mary's and we weren't pals. It wasn't a competing church yet you'd wonder why they put two churches right next door to each other. We came to understand that St. Mary's was essentially built to accommodate the growing tribe that had settled in Knightsville from Itri, Italy and St. Ann's was for everybody else. About the time we started driving, St. Mary's got a cool young priest that you could actually listen to and he'd get you out on time as well. The Catholic youth caught on to this guy and soon there were too many non-paying seats being taken at St. Mary's and the pastor actually blocked the door:

"You kids don't belong here; go to your own church".

It was the only time I ever heard a priest say that a Catholic needed to leave His church and it was the last time I ever cared about missing Mass. Then we spent Sunday mornings at Mr. Donut rehearsing lies to tell Mom. Cool young priest went on to stand with the accused.

A guy named Joseph Smith goes into the woods and has a conversation with God and God gives him some golden tablets with all of the rules written on them. Then God takes the tablets back and tells Joseph Smith to go forth and preach about everything he has just witnessed. He must lead all those men that he can convince and all the women that they would marry out of harm's way to eventually settle in Salt Lake City and live happily ever after without alcohol or coffee. Enough of them willingly did so and they out - begatted the gentiles and overran the Native Americans and now they rule all of Utah through Gerry Mandering, the 13th apostle. Joseph kept at it until he lost his life to an angry mob of skeptics - never even made it to Utah - and then Brigham Young took over. They built a huge temple and then many more and every community got a substation that they call a "stakehouse" or a "wardhouse". The upside is that the Mormons take care of the poorest among them. The downside is that Mormons are assessed ten per cent of what they report to the IRS. Strictly supervised youngsters who are called "elders" are dispatched throughout the world to champion the cause, though I couldn't tell you what goes into deciding who goes to Zurich or Vienna and who goes to South America. The populace is governed by rationing access to the temple and the temple is never open to the general public except for that very special period just after completion. Looks like a funeral home or a mansion to me. The women of the sect hold no ecclesiastic influence and the acceptance of color is only recent history. There is no longer any polygamy except for where there really is while the church fails to evolve in a world where coffee is now considered an antioxidant and you still can't get a proper cocktail. Amen.

In the end, I just want to know to Whom I should properly give thanks because I have enjoyed the best of everything I ever wanted.

I don't blame anybody's god for my own inadequacies nor do I covet the women or the worldly goods of others. Never did. Nor do I understand how Christianity and Capitalism are supposed to co-exist without a conflict of purpose. Ted Haggard and his ilk would have you believe that everybody who isn't evangelical like them is destined for the eternal fire, re-hab from homosexual behavior notwithstanding. Kind of makes you wonder if a work in progress is allowed any grace at all. Of all my religious education, the most dramatic influence on me was a cartoon of a guy standing alone at the pearly gates, looking over his shoulder. St. Peter says to him:

"What made you think there was a line?"

How They All Died

Dad had himself a beauty of a heart attack at the farm, far away from any immediate medical aid. By the time rescue got him to the ER he was so critical that he spent the rest of the night suspended in Trendelenberg* to maintain his blood pressure until emergency bi-pass could be performed. Once again Dr. Singh made it look easy but not for Carolyn. She was on the unit, comforting Mom and trying to remain entirely above the fray that our family situation always seemed to present. In a private and sober moment with Carolyn, Dad broke down and promised to put our family back together. Upon his discharge Dad thanked Carolyn for her assistance and walked out of Rhode Island Hospital. Nothing changed except that he had to quit smoking.

DejaVu all over again; a few weeks out Dad has chest pain once again and the family tried to drive him to RIH. They divert to Station 4 where I'm working off shift and Steven appears in the doorway between the day room and the rescue bay:

"My father's having a heart attack!!!"

We leap to our feet and I'm the first one out to the car and he's awake and breathing. My friend Doug is driving rescue that night and now he's right by my side and our very first priority is to get Dad to the truck. The old protocols would have it that you do at least an abbreviated work-up in place, but all of us know that the rescue truck is the rolling ER where everything is available and wieldy. I ask about his pain in detail and I wonder if he'll even answer and I don't even take notice of Mom.

Not everybody knows about me and Dad and throughout this episode, no one even knows that this *is* Dad - so I don't tell 'em, either. We get him on the monitor, some 02, and Doug runs down an I.V line. I prep Dad for the stick and I look to see him staring blankly at the ceiling.

"The last time, the other guy couldn't see a vein.
He didn't even try."

"Yeah, well that was him..."

The needle goes right in and we have a patent line which translates into access for meds. The EKG displays the rhythm of an elderly heart but Dad is only 53. I'm relieved that I only have to worry about keeping a pulse for the next ten minutes. I take a breath and sit back and realize there's Mom, nestled in the corner of the truck - not leaving Dad, ever. I look right at her:

"He's O.K."

Mom says nothing, and her steely gaze offers no acknowledgement that she even heard me. All the way to the hospital we are silent while I pretend to be busy running off EKG strips and fuss with the I.V. while I watch Dad's every twitch. He is still fixated upon the ceiling – never looked at me; not once. I wonder what he must have thought about having his nit wit son responsible for his well being just then.

We let them off at the ER where Mom follows the stretcher and I don't even look back. Doug and I set about to restore the truck to get back in service.

"Did you know those people?"
"Yeah. Why?"
"I don't know – it just seemed like you knew them."
"It was my mother and father."

Doug looked right at me:
"But how did you...?"
"We ain't close."

You make allowances for the shortcomings in those you love, but sometimes you allow too much. When it happens too often, you re-negotiate how much is too often. When something gets to be a little too severe, you re-negotiate that also. Retreat means even more retreat until you either won't do it any more or commit to doing it forever. Mom was all about retreat; the tidal wave that carried her off had a pretty easy time of it because Mom was always afraid of the water.

It probably wasn't anybody's fault when Mom inexplicably died. The medical minds were happy enough to indict a vendor because Dad wanted a lawsuit and the failure needed a name. Mom's unfortunate life would have only been about more of the same; even when we were little, we used to listen to her pray to be taken. Gram took the loss quietly but Gramp was inconsolable. For once, Dad had little to say.

We didn't invite the kids to endure the funeral since KJ hadn't seen anybody for so long and Bobby barely knew any of the cast. Me and Carolyn and David and Suzi stepped up to the funeral home and to the receiving line like everyone else paying their respects who wasn't family. Jazzy glared and stood with the twins as Dad held out his empty heart and lifeless hand for me to entertain.

"You can be here with the family, if you want..."

" I don't think so..."

They had set up four chairs for four people and it wasn't us.

I was all the way across town stationed in Edgewood when the call came in for a building fire at Gramp's house. I pretty much figured it would be the shop because it was overflowing with everything Gramp never got rid of and his idea of a fire extinguisher was two gallons of milk jug water. True enough, the rickety old cast iron wood stove got a little too hot and ignited all of the scrap that was a little too close. They declared a code red but they fought the fire out of the tank and called out a rescue for Gramp. Seems he got a little excited.

We met Rescue 2 at the ER at Rhode Island Hospital where I got every assurance that Gramp was mostly O.K. No family had yet arrived so it was just me and Gramp, who told me all about how his heart "went off like trip hammer". He pulled out his wallet and handed me the hundred dollar bill to hold that he had kept squirreled away because "your grandmother doesn't know about this one..." From the ER, he eventually went home until he had another bout of chest pain that he'd finally admit to. They took Gramp to a private ER and then to a catholic hospital where he was mis-diagnosed and ended up back at RIH. There, he went upstairs for a cardiac cath where he showed everyone how to survive a 95% blockage of his left main coronary artery - the widowmaker. In short order, Dr. Singh opened Gramp's chest and worked his magic and Carolyn stayed at his side and everything got to be O.K. for a while. But later on Gramp couldn't swallow easily and then he couldn't swallow at all. The cancer surgery was ugly and painful and couldn't erase all those years of too many cigars. Gramp finally died in the nursing home right after I last saw him, which was really a week after I thought that he wouldn't make it through that very night. He was mostly comatose by then, with a festering bedsore that ran the length of his anterior. I thought of how he should have just dropped dead from the fire and avoided the miracles of modern medicine. Throughout his suffering, Gram was quiet and demure.

Me and David and the next-door cousins drove Gramp's Caddy through the city to St. Ann's Church and through St. Ann's

Cemetery to the chapel where they receive the casket. After we all left, they probably slid the box right out the back and onto a truck that would plop Gramp into a hole just like me and KJ used to watch them do, all those years ago. He would lie next to or on top of Mom, depending on how they arrange a reservation for four but I kind of hope that its' Gram who got laid out next to Dad. They pretty much despised each other, and Gramp really loved his daughter.

Everybody felt for Mom and helped Mom wherever they could when the twins were little, especially if Dad wasn't around. One of the aunts had serious words with Dad over how he could just arrogantly dismiss everybody's feelings. She had Dad pegged and she came right at him and still kept up her friendship with Mom until Dad and then Gram made a mess of it. Gram was still always Mom's best friend, probably because Mom was so malleable. Another aunt had plenty of words *about* Dad when he'd fire up something loud at six o'clock on a Sunday morning. Her husband had to maintain both sides of the hedge that separated our yard from theirs because Dad wouldn't give a rat's rear end about how it all looked. As soon as their kids were grown and gone, aunt and uncle moved to another zip code, just for the view.

All of the cousins did well enough - educated, motivated, productive. Most of them honor their parents, belong to a church, and help out with civic duties. They married well and raised nice families and we never get invited to see many of them at once. Of the whole combined family there's only one 'ner do well and he's one of ours. He mimicked Dad in every deceivable way and personalized a few more, just to offend the rest of us. We were wrong to take away his motorcycle when we did because we cost him that first fortune in not getting himself crippled. Everybody seems happy enough that he has yet to acknowledge any progeny.

Jazzy was the only thread of our being that pushed its' way through the familial fabric. Jazzy could identify each aged relative without resorting to dental records and she was useful in reintroducing me and David to everybody we didn't know throughout the funerals. I hadn't gone to many of the clan weddings which seemed to come one after the other during my troubles with soon to be exWife. Jazzy took enough interest in so many nuptials that now she knows everybody's kids as well. I've only been to three weddings that ever mattered, the second one being Sophie's where I first fell for Carolyn.

I seriously thought about changing my last name in honor of Gramp but really it would have been in dishonor of Dad. It was uncharted territory in the history of obstinate Larrivees to offer up such an insult but if someone had put the paper in front of me, I'd have turned Caito in an instant. Carolyn's son Bobby changed his last name to Bonniol, ostensibly to perpetuate the brand in the person of his own son, Tristan. Ol' Jimbo got just what he deserved out of that and we were proud of the kid for doing it. It doesn't matter how nicely it was all explained - that's a bell you can't un-ring.

Turning Caito probably still wouldn't have made me an heir to any of Gramp's fortune. That was all pretty well established before Dad could even get involved. Dad used to say that Gram could come to stay with them if she'd just agree to sign over all they were worth, but the rest of the Caito's helped Gram to out live Dad at the other zip code. The Larrivee's got invited to the yard sale after they emptied Gram out of the house but Dad was years gone by thèn. Jazzy spoke for all of us when she told off one of the aunts for taking everything of value and finally, we just left the remains of our life with Gram and Gramp to strangers.

There was no such calamity when Dad died. We had heard that he was ill and that they had traced his brain tumor to a kidney cancer that apparently had gone asymptomatic until it blossomed. By then it was all a foregone conclusion except for Dad who maintained throughout that the doctors said he would be cured. We had never renewed any kind of an association with Dad and got all this information second hand. But even the family who had despised Dad's behavior for all those years were now feeling sorry for him since he now had almost no one and he looked so awful. There were whisperings about a girlfriend and after Dad's funeral it was discovered that all of Mom's heirloom jewelry would never be handed down to Jazzy. My Eagle Scout medal that Mom so treasured apparently went the same way. The estate was cash poor and property taxes on the farm were due.

As soon as I heard that Dad had a brain tumor, I penned a letter that included none of the rancor, none of the disaffection I had embodied since childhood. I asked that he consider Jazzy, that his only daughter who may or may not always have just enough should be entitled to a better future. There would be no reply - just a snide remark that would find its way to the author of such an ignominious request. Dad went his way, lashing out at any and all who would enter his terminal existence. Nearing his end, one of the aunts reported seeing Dad in the church he had almost never attended - a ghastly specter of the man everybody used to fear.

I had predicted exactly the day of Dad's death. It was easy since we had been carefully orchestrating a European ski trip, kids included. It was the biggest thing we would ever do with them; even my son agreed to go. Dad would die three days before our scheduled departure so that I could cave to everybody's expectations and call off the trip. Didn't happen; I stuck to the plan I had laid in my own mind months before. It came down to whether or not I would subject my wife and kids to missing out so that I could dutifully pretend to pay homage to a man I cared nothing more about. It was a no-brainer and while several people might have attended Dad's wake, we were on a plane. For my son, there should have been a lesson there somewhere.

There was a will that did not name three of Mom and Dad's five children and it was entirely by design. Nearing his end, Dad tried desperately to force a settlement from the litigation about Mom's death so that it could be passed on to Dad and thusly, to Dad's estate. Dad's attorneys weren't willing to settle for a percentage of so much less and Dad died during the conflict. By law, anybody who would have been a principal at probate is required to be notified of the proceedings, just as though the decedents had died intestate. We all got the same letters including the one where we were invited to sign away any rights we might have had in exchange for a dollar. For reasons known only to Jazzy and the twins, the other side got Jazzy to agree. David and I hired a sharp estate attorney who entered an appearance on our behalf and brought everything to a screeching halt. The six figure settlement went into escrow and Jazzy called to express in plain language her opinion of what we were doing:

"They didn't want us to have anything
and none of us deserve any!"

Then she offered to kill me off if I got in the way of any of it.

Shortly before Mom died but long after Dad had promised to get right with everybody, they had decided to address the issues of who should not inherit. It was reported that Mom wouldn't sign on unless Jazzy was also excluded and apparently Dad decided that this was one promise that he could keep. The whip-smart lawyer for me and David held the product liability settlement hostage until the twins couldn't disagree any longer. Me and David cut Jazzy in for a third which was 100% more than she ever would have gotten, then we bought new jeans. After Dad's funeral, the twins were cleaning out the freezer where they found a pile of money stuffed in an envelope that Jazzy would still never see.

Gram died the year before me and Carolyn left for the west. She had outlived Mom and Dad and Gramp by a number of years and now Gram was late of nowhere in particular. Gram had been in a nursing home for years, locked away as people are who have worn out their welcome or outlived their usefulness but not their money. Gone would be the manifestations of pride and purpose, breathing on as longevity would have it. Gram had become malformed and demented and my sister who had been the medical professional could not contain her distain for the quality of Gram's care. She soon found herself barred from the place, a written order duly signed and witnessed.

Gram's funeral was the capstone of an enduring regime that had become a part of our past long ago. There are memories of Gram's kindness to the Larrivee children, the children of her only daughter and perhaps Gram's only true friend. We could always just walk in on Gram during the day. You'd get a treat but it came with a lecture; Gram was always well stocked with both. What others would define as criticism, Gram considered merely correction. How deservedly one could hold one's head up was *the* one treasured value that Gram seemed to live for. If Gramp ever told a joke or a story with even a hint of blue, she'd be all over him for it. He'd smile and she'd implode so as not to display any excess of her indignation. It would be a pretty good harrumph just the same if you knew what to look for. I suspect that Gramp didn't get a whole lot of what most men truly enjoy and I'll bet he got plenty of what we don't. Propriety was everything to Gram; affection, not so much.

The dutiful got to drive from the church, through the cemetery, and on to the chapel that I would enter for the very last time. The new engraving on the headstone would fade with time so now it looks as though everybody died in order until you get up close. Then you'd have to wonder about the tragedy that befell this family.

RESCUE YOU

I can get a little intense about my career with the real fire department. I have taken and shown great pride in what we did for people but I have also known deep regret and disappointment. Anything from the "coulda', woulda', shoulda' file would qualify in any case where somebody's life was dramatically changed. A rescue company officer is responsible for doing all the right things in exactly the right order and as quickly as possible to avert impending disaster. That is the gold standard. Others along the path to recovery will have their own opportunity to make a mess of things, but that part shouldn't begin in the field. How well I lived up to what I profess here is for everybody else to judge, especially since I've been so judgmental of others. I don't apologize for castigating people who didn't care about what our mission was, and I like to think I drove off a few who didn't belong. Thankfully, those people don't stay with rescue anyway.

I got some good mentoring early on from Hawkins and Nottel, paying more attention than they ever knew. After I first got promoted, I had to think for myself and for the patient, more than I had ever realized since Pelico and I had been such a team. Dave Fecteau - who was a fellow rescue lieutenant - helped to settle me down when one particular call went especially bad. An old guy had expired but he was warm enough to work on when his wife suddenly started having chest pain. I called for a second rescue and Dave showed up on Rescue 2 for the wife while my own emergency was going so awfully bad. Nothing was working out; we couldn't get an airway, we couldn't get an I.V. going, and the guy was getting to be room temperature. Out of the house and into the truck, Dave jumps in. He'd been doing this for a while and he was as collected as Hawkins:

"Let's make this look like it's supposed to."

And together we set about to do so. It was all Dave ever said about my abject failure in that case and no one ever had to say it to me again. Me and Dave weren't close - friendly enough but not pals - yet he stood me right up. The episode got me to realize that exasperation is not a solution to any such dilemma. The guys who seemed cool actually *were* cool and however you come by it, you cannot do this job any other way.

When I got hired by the Cranston Fire Department, I'd have bet anybody a week's pay or more that they'd have to carry me off the job kicking and screaming. That was back when I really thought I knew everything. Since then I have come to understand that circumstances do in fact get to be out of control and that the human condition can indeed be worn out. No one who is 25 or so would agree. *"Gettin' old aint't for sissies"* used to be just a geezer mantra but I could feel it coming at 35. Some people like Captain Brown got rode really hard and seemed to walk right through it while some of us got hurt once or twice and never fully recovered. Fitness counts a great deal but injury happens anyway and the real challenge is to stay out of surgery and away from the pills.

Some of what essentially drove me off was too many nights wasted on old people who couldn't poop or who thought that they must be ill since they were awake at 3 A.M. There would be plenty of other nonsense that causes people to call 911. Even the simplest calls could eat up an hour and often times, something serious would come in that you couldn't take because you were tied up with stupid. People need to look in on their elderly a whole lot more than they do. Towards the end I was telling people to call "119".

"Don't you mean 911?"

"No ma'am – call 119; we come faster."

There were incidents that would leave a lasting impression; indelible stories that you just never get over. Some are very sad. There was never any such thing as treatment for post-traumatic stress disorder until much later in my career. By then, I was way too far into how I dealt with my sensitive side to ever agree to needing any help. None of us would even recognize it if we *did* need employee assistance since we always had the guys on our shift to set us straight. When John Nottell got to be Deputy Chief of Rescue, he quietly made everybody aware that help was available and that by law it was confidential. It was highly commendable of John the way he went about it but I don't know of anybody who took any confidential help, so maybe it really was confidential. Hard to imagine on the real fire department, where rumor and gossip reside. I also never knew anybody who was mentally ill that would actually *admit* to it but then, people deny all kinds of reality. Not me. It's kind of like Altzeimer's disease - if you think you have it then you probably don't. But we all knew who the nut cases were.

What emergency medicine did to me - to all of us - was make us hardened and people around me have suffered for it. It makes you grow up in a hurry and ages you even faster. It takes the precious out of life right before your very eyes, like a soldier weary of battle would see. What happens accidentally and incidentally and intentionally is thrust right at you until everything that should be decidedly different soon becomes routine. We had to take an indifferent approach to human suffering in order to improve upon the situation at hand and after a while, you get to where you can just wash off the remains and get back to lunch. By extension, you become a whole lot less sympathetic to what some people would perceive as serious, and that would include immediate family. Carolyn, as an ER nurse, perfectly understood but the kids remained clueless by choice. Me and Carolyn were blessed with healthy children who had never suffered serious mishap. Despite the stories that followed me home, our children never considered the misfortune of others. I would come to resent their ignorance:

"I know about hunger; I watched my friend Thomas be hungry".

It's easy to appreciate (or resent) how good your own kids have it after you get to see how some others must live. We took a call off of Laurel Hill Avenue one day to find a gramma who was the sole support and caregiver of a brain damaged child. The little boy could make monkey noises and flail about some but there was no sign of coherency or recognition - just a vacant stare. The medical history was extensive and rescue was called because the kid had a shunt in his brain and was days into a fever that wouldn't break. Gramma went on to explain that her daughter couldn't bear to allow this child to die at birth the way that the medical people explained that he should. Then she abandoned the whole scene, leaving the gramma to do what she could with just a little help from the state. Gramma would never leave this child's side, convinced as she was that there was some example of intellect yet to be found in her charge.

Closer to home, we had Billy Kerwin. Billy's mother was tragically killed by a truck and then his father foolishly un-corked a steaming radiator and died from the sepsis of third degree burns. Billy lived with his gramma and she was pretty strict and she caught Billy with a little contraband and chased him up a tree with a stick. A branch in the upper reaches broke and Billy fell straight down and broke his shoulder where he really should have broken his neck. We wrapped him to go and when we next looked in on him at the hospital, Billy lay suspended in upper body cast and traction with his gramma sitting close by, still nagging at him. Billy knew our kids - they were all early teens - and I used to see him around all the time but as bad as that kid ever had it, he was always pleasant and happy enough. Our kids were mostly miserable because they both wanted to be Peter Sean.

Peter Sean was the only child of my good friend Peter Pan who drove Ladder 1 on our shift. Peter Pan was long and lean and bright and amusing and he defied any and all signs of aging. He wooed younger women and he drove a Porche and he was familiar to all of Pawtuxet Village and some of their daughters. Peter Sean lived with his mom across the street from us and later on, just around the corner so we used to see him all the time. Our kids would point to Peter Sean as *the* living example of how they thought they should be treated – nice car, nice clothes, nice life. The part they conveniently left out was *nice kid,* because Peter Sean always carried himself as an extraordinary young man - polite, respectable, studious. Peter the elder took no credit for the goodness in his son and would always say that Peter Sean was raised well by his mother. Me and Carolyn would quite agree and say also that Peter Sean displayed a subtle but classier degree of courtesy and cool than even his dad could manage.

At about the time we were looking at Bob getting behind the wheel, there was a spectacular crash on Wilbur Avenue where three kids drove a Chevy wagon just like ours into a utility pole at high speed. It was such a direct hit that the front tag was curled perfectly around the pole along with the bumper. The pole sheared in two and the whole of the front of the car was pushed all the way back to the firewall. The vehicle caught fire, two of the kids were trapped, and of the three, only one survived. Budlong was the Rescue Captain at Station 4 at the time and he was first due and he called a whole second alarm response with the Jaws of Life and special signaled a third rescue which was us, all the way over in Edgewood. We took the kid who survived and he was burned and broken and bloodied beyond recognition. The next day, on a rainy Sunday morning I took our two over to Sal Zincone's salvage yard where they had taken the car. We walked around the wreck several times as the kids peered through where the windows had been while I described in detail what had happened. There was blood, there were beer cans and there was catastrophe in somebody else's household. It was probably the very first time our kids ever got to see what we worked with and they may even have been mightily impressed because there was only a deferential silence and the rain. I related about how nobody had ever looked ahead to see how this could happen and that the alcohol had only confounded everybody's judgment. Both sons would go on to imbibe more than the law allows but just this once, nobody had any rebuttal.

When I first came face to face with a victim of HIV, it was an unforeseen moment from back when I had no idea of how I should behave except as a professional. It was right around the time that Freddie Mercury died which I remember well because I wanted to slap silly the guy who photographed poor Freddie on his deathbed. Then I thought about what a great shot it was, how even if the guy was holding a gun, it wouldn't have mattered to Freddie. My first AIDS guy was a drug addict who could have been a twin to my friend Broadway Billy who also had some dependency issues. It was what they now call "a teaching moment" since I saw Billy's face, also.

The guy met us at the door on Carmen St. and insisted on walking to the truck. He was burning with fever and his lungs weren't clear and the first thing he told us was that he had AIDS as in:

> "Guys.. I'm tellin' ya up front that I got AIDS from when I did drugs and I ain't queer or nuthin' like that".

We took him into the back of the rescue truck and dismissed the engine company and put on gloves. We put the guy on oxygen with a non re-breather mask like they never inflate on TV and decided that the I.V. wasn't worth the time, the trouble, or the exposure. If he was in any kind of distress we'd have certainly gone the other way but cooling off his brain was far more indicated and

I would still do exactly as we had. And if he was queer, it wouldn't have mattered.

We never got any direction from Dad about queer behavior because he never spoke of it. Hardly anyone did. Since nobody was "out" in any way, shape or form, there wasn't anything more than private musings. You wouldn't want any of it to be about you if you weren't gay but I imagine those who really were gay didn't care unless they felt threatened. There was none of that through high school unless I completely missed it and I was shocked to learn that somewhere between one and two out of every ten people are gay. And gay people could be cowboys or race car drivers or fighter pilots or rescue guys just like me; they ain't all hairdressers. Even in college during the radical days, you never gave it a thought while you were gazing at every leggy coed. The gays must have been finding each other through some indeterminate network; an underground railroad for those who understood. But one or two out of every ten got people to scrutinizing each other a little more closely and it brought out the worst of American prejudice. Some people think it's O.K. to judge others as aberrant and therefore deserving of the justice that the Lord thy God would administer through their very own hand. Others truly believe that AIDS is the just dessert of sinners so afflicted who also have no need or desire to repent. Dad might have agreed with all of that and more but he also seemed satisfied enough that none of his kids were even remotely queer, as though he would ever know. Turns out, one likely is.

HIV brought out the warmongering in gay and straight alike. The bias needed a banner and the militants of each side sought allies. Most people weren't sure how they should feel since it might involve their own kids or other people whom they loved. God's people branded homosexuality an aberration that could be reduced or cured altogether with prayer while the other side sought safety in numbers large enough to matter. Civil rights would take on a much larger role since this now affected white people. Gay bias would divide the Bush/Cheney crowd, Cheney's daughter being amongst the stricken. In our house, it wasn't discussed and it mostly didn't matter, even when Bob took up with the theatre life. Gay women lived next door and we were pals and even their male friends were nice enough so where's the problem? Our kids threatened our marriage more than any couple of gays that I ever knew.

The Beginning of the End

I grew up the oldest child of a bully who had sewn a field of fear that went on for as far as anyone could see and for as long as anyone could remember. Even Dad's pals saw what was happening to us kids, but if anybody ever stepped up to tell him so, I never heard about it. Breathing was chosen over rebellion and there would never be a police report about Dad's first born. When I no longer feared death at Dad's hand, the relationship largely ended. Dad's first grandchild had other ideas about what a responsible childhood would not entail and his only remorse ever would be about getting caught. Our older boy tried to take some cue from Dad's first grandchild because my son made it look so cool and easy. Mostly what Bob got was the retribution.

It was a mistake to expect an older brother/younger brother nurturing affair within our habitat. We were raising two dissimilar and solitary children who would seldom acknowledge any acceptance of each other except for when it served their very own selves. There was precious little to savor as they took us from one adventure to the next, usually having to do with cars, beer, obfuscation and the law. Bob, although a few years older, still had a little manhood to catch up on since he had only had his mother's influence for so long. My son had always had his mother and his father and he never felt he needed anybody else. Carolyn knew that right from the outset and she never tried to supplant exWife. Carolyn was good and kind and fair, even when it meant that she had to disagree with me in favor of either of our two. No good deed by her ever went unpunished.

We started out well enough, not counting how sick everybody got at the wedding. We returned safely from London to find David and Suzi re-thinking the idea of children after a week with ours.

Rusty was overjoyed to see us while the kids were decidedly resentful over what had apparently befallen them. They embarked upon a couple of years of pushing and shoving and trying to out do each other with unabridged distemper. There was little order and even less accountability as I was overruled at nearly every stringent objection while the boys got to turn a deaf ear. Me and Carolyn were soon at odds and everything to do with the kids had to be a negotiated settlement. There was plenty of room for misconception and plenty of opportunity to create it and there was always the other parent.

Bob had it worse by far because he would rebel within the privacy of himself while he outwardly rejected any reasonable influence. Bob kicked his own ass enough that I didn't have to except that sometimes I did anyway. He was the oldest except for when he failed to act the part and that kept him from behind the wheel for an extra year. Bob would almost silently endure my fits of intemperance because in a nod to Dad, I've always had diplomacy issues, a degree of sordid impatience and I don't suffer foolish waste at all. Or thievery, which caused us to have to put a passage lock on our bedroom door because one or both couldn't refrain from a little self indulgence.

My son allowed for only his own authority over himself, almost from the time he escaped his crib. Mom and Dad would remark that my "little man" didn't need to be an adult or treated as such quite so soon. Little did they know that it would never be up to me - that I could only choose between beating him down like Dad would or letting him think for himself. We had been brought up to believe in Dad Almighty who would provide and protect - so long as you did what Dad said. But Dad would abscond of any obligation promised or implied and always without explanation or justification. Dad screwed Steven pretty good, promising a full ride to wherever Steven chose to take a college education. He even said it in front of Uncle Steve the Austrian, creating a foregone conclusion for the only one of Dad's children who would ever graduate from college. Then he hardly helped at all. My kid would be raised quite the opposite, schooled in standing for himself and in doing for himself and becoming a partner in the life we would always share. Our life together took a decidedly different turn as my son decided that we should just tolerate his "acting out" and pony up to his expectations. KJ became sullen and silent and he created an agenda of his own. There would always be new adventures in parenting to cherish:

Santi's dad used to walk up and down Park Ave. wearing a cashmere overcoat in the simmering heat while pounding himself in the head. He spoke jibberish and he got agitated if anybody tried to help him so mostly, everybody left him alone. He wouldn't see a doctor and by the time he sustained a seizure and his brain tumor was diagnosed, it was much too late. My son and an accomplice saw this as an opportunity to admit themselves to Santi's house, probably just because they could. They were young and impertinent and they had no idea of the consequences had they been caught red-handed, especially by an addled homeowner. They were seen and identified by a party who was kind enough and brave enough to notify me. I summoned my son to the bedroom where he summarily got to look down the wrong end of the twelve gauge. I screamed at him:

"WHAT THE HELL ARE YOU DOING IN MY HOUSE!!"

"Now imagine – I'm a crazy guy who doesn't love you".

I remain truly sorry that I broke my son's tooth but he never should have told his friends that his father was afraid of him:

"My father does what *I* tell him…
if he knows what's good for him"

We had casually said to no one in particular that we were

going out to pick up a movie. That was mistakenly heard as "we were going *to the movies*" and of course we came right back. My son decided, as he had apparently been doing right along, that he had a couple of hours to go joyriding with a friend in the family wagon. He was just 15 and had no license or authority to do any such thing. We returned from Major Video to discover the wagon missing and we knew that Bob was elsewhere and so I called the Cranston Police. The cops put out a citywide APB describing the car and right away the beat cop called in to say that he had just accosted the pair; two kids sitting on the tailgate of the wagon, pondering what to do next. The cop stopped by our house to explain how it went:

"License and registration, please."

And my kid, cool as you please:

" I'm Gerry Larrivee's son – you know him – Lieutenant on rescue...."

And he was polite and well-meaning and hadn't done anything wrong, so the cop just let him go. I was furious that my son was making such asses of us all but the greater priority was about finding the kid and the car, hopefully intact. He had to know we were home and that we knew what had happened so I began to search an expanding radius from our house. Soon enough, I spotted my son and his pal walking up Lakeside Ave. like they had no idea.

"Where's the car?!!" I demanded.

"What car? I don't have the car".

I jumped out of my truck and threw him up against it so hard that he almost fell into the bed. I dragged him around to the other side and made him get in next to me. By now the friend is well on his way; I don't even know who he was.

"Where's the goddam car?!!"

"I don't have the car!!"

CRACK!!

It was only supposed to be a little backhand but there might have been some exasperation and a knuckle behind it.

"Ooh! My tooth; my tooth!!"

"Where's the goddam car?!!"

"I'll show you; I'll show you!!"

We go home where I make nice with the cops and there are no charges brought against my son or the cop who had let him go. Me and Carolyn go pick up the wagon and the only real harm is to the perpetrator himself. The next day, I take my son and the remains of his incisor to Melvin who is the best dentist who ever lived. Since the break is distal to anything important, Melvin simply glues the tooth back together without question or comment or even a trace of fracture. We really liked Melvin.

One time, they both went to a party nearby in Edgewood. Somebody needed to be picked up in Pawtuxet, down near the water, and my under-age son wrangles the keys from Bob. On the way back, he sideswipes a parked car and chooses to drive on but a guy across the street - a lawyer - sees it from his front porch and races out to the street. He tries to obstruct my get-away son and apparently has to leap clear to keep from being hit but he gets the plate number just the same. Bob and KJ then conspire to abandon the vehicle and report it stolen so that there would be some confusion over the time frame of what had happened except that there wasn't. Upon his arrest, my son is charged with ASSAULT WITH A DEADLY WEAPON. More charges arise from the false police report and it starts to look like we need a lawyer and a number of zeros assigned to a check. Didn't happen. A friend in a high place steps in and hard comeuppance is off the table. It helps that KJ has no juvenile record, but not because he's innocent. ExWife and I get to share an uncomfortable audience with an officer of the court who directs my son to hug his parents who love him so and the ASSAULT WITH A DEADLY WEAPON charge disappears. Kumbaya.

The end of my son's innocence was now upon us. The local junior high school was full of incorrigible youth, practicing delinquency while the administration looked away by choice. We knew that we had to move beyond the public school system that had deteriorated noticeably since my days there. Bob was struggling; granted he was largely unmotivated by academic achievement but he got no real help there, either. We decided that Bishop Hendricken High School would be the perfect environment for my son to focus on his education and his athletics without the distraction of gangland politics or a pretty young lab partner. The school was founded and operated by the Congregation of Christian Brothers, an ancient Catholic society originating in Ireland. Theology was a mandatory part of the curriculum, and the former in-laws were thrilled. Even ex-Wife got on board and agreed to pay for some of it. Although he would never shine scholastically, my son did well enough at Hendricken to justify the choice of leaving public school behind.

Even the good times came with issues. If a ski trip happened to fall on exWife's weekend there would be a situation not with her but with KJ. Baseball should have been a nurturing rite of passage, but exWife also attended the games. Although we kept our distance, there was a palpable discomfort and when exWife took up with another kid's much older Dad, there was more than a little commentary. When my son was chosen to play baseball in the senior league, I was especially dis-invited to have any part of it so I stayed away. When some friends were taking their kids to Fenway, my son wouldn't go. This was the same kid who got to spend overnights in the fire station whenever exWife bailed on short notice. How much of this was just being a teenager and how much of this was decidedly a bias against myself is anybody's guess. I don't think I really knew my son.

For me and Carolyn, the most gratifying time of our first years together came after one of our unfortunate subjects fled with our blessing into the arms of the other parent. Not wishing to remain alone and vulnerable to our care, the other chose the same. Both boys had committed to an unrelenting stalemate when I refused to finish the upstairs bedrooms beyond bare floors and sheetrock until they could learn to simply pick up after themselves. They responded by living even more like vermin until they realized that the trash cans were full of *their* belongings headed for the curb. An agreement was struck whereby the exes' would once again become parents and soon the upstairs was empty. One son left to share a bedroom with a pair of toddlers while the other set about to get between exWife and her next husband. For me and Carolyn, it was a taste of the future we had never dared to imagine and it was fun while it lasted. Shortly after the upstairs was nicely furnished, the boys returned and all was as before.

The college years brought home to us the upward mobility our sons would fashion for themselves without actually having to work for it. Clueless as any parents then or since, we brushed aside the warning signs of our little college wannabes and let them take charge. Bob had spent time hanging out at Brown University (where he left a trail of Chevy wagon parts) and we actually wasted a couple of hundred dollars on an application for admission. After we depleted all of his college account on remedial studies at

Roger Williams College, Bob went on to Rhode Island College to pursue a life in the theatre arts.

My son would campaign relentlessly for admission to Bentley College which at the time was in the top two on somebody's list of business schools with tuition commensurate with that rating. I was against the idea because the other business college in the top two was Bryant College which was about 20 minutes away, half the cost, and I had a friend sitting on the board. Carolyn argued that my son had held up his end scholastically and therefore deserved the opportunity to direct our immediate future. Wasn't this why we had enrolled him at Hendricken?

Neither child would ever put a pen to a scholarship application - couldn't be bothered to even try for one. To pay for the Bentley College Experience I created a company called:

J.B. SeaCo - Exterior Restoration, Maintenance & Repair

The name came from Gramp's "JBC" initials because he had taught all of us the value of quality workmanship and because I admired him so.

"Never enough time to do it right; always enough time
to do it over" He'd say.

The idea was to gainfully, lucratively – employ my son so that he could do a little better than bag groceries for minimum wage. We painted houses, cut grass, re-built fences; anything that was outside work. I learned to use epoxy to restore wooden gutters and wooden boats so that you'd never know they had been rotted through. I took every available hour of overtime the fire department offered while my son fought me over his share of the business that I had insisted we put in the bank. The splits were all very simple since we cut the business three ways: a third for education, another third for education, and a third to pay for overhead and a living allowance for KJ through the summer. The college financing came from First Wachovia which was a fair and responsible lender at the time. We paid for the first semester and we co-signed for the second with an interest-only loan that required a balloon payment at the end. That loan could be converted to a conventional loan if you were good enough at paying back the bank. We also had the original college account exWife and I had started all those years ago that she said I had foolishly rolled over into a CD that paid a mere 11 point something per cent for four years. We used that to cover the magic laptop that the school sold separately.

Our Larrivees' have historically learned through necessity at an early age about how to come by enough dollars. Our children did not, choosing instead to ignore pragmatism or learn at anybody's knee the very basics of economic common sense. Your wants are many, your needs are few and so it follows that you address the needs first and sometimes not just your own. Too much month at the end of the money ain't just a country song. Income hadn't kept up with inflation and every middle class American family of that time was either learning to do without or they were up to their eyeballs in debt. It was the 80's. Greed was good for some - everybody else bought on the credit that our kids learned to abuse while the bankers egged us on. Then the bankers showed their patriotic side with new fees and exorbitant usury terms and our congress signed on with both hands open wide. For me and Carolyn, the IRS would come to depend on our two professional incomes; you could never hide a dime.

Mark Patinkin is a newspaper columnist at the Providence Journal who should have won a Pulitzer for his work about world hunger that got us to giving more. But one time he wrote a column about how much water he didn't waste when the sink was disconnected underneath to empty into a bucket, and how fast that bucket filled up if you weren't careful. It's the same as being in a hole; just stop digging. Our kids eventually got to qualify for all the stuff they never knew they needed. Enter one other parent who taught that relief was just another credit card away and fiscal responsibility was only for people who had real money to protect. Another parent got stiffed pretty good for playing the hero and it snagged the kid's credit rating as well.

We had gotten Bob a car; a yellow '67 Plymouth Barracuda coupe that an old guy had hung on to after his wife died. It was her car and you could tell that he was really torn about letting it go but there was no good to come from letting it just sit there. The car was immaculate, and the Slant 6 that powered it was faster in the 80's than almost anything the other kids were driving to school. It was the same motor I had in my '65 fastback except that it had a Torqueflite automatic that shifted faster than a stick, so I might even have lost that race. The yellow Barracuda didn't last long. Bob aspired to Yuppie-dom and a little square Honda that his dad was looking to unload. Bob could just take over the payments and the comprehensive insurance package that would be required and I would stay out of the arrangement. We sold the Barracuda for enough to cover some of the insurance but I don't really know how much of that loan ever got paid. The Honda leaked oil and the motor burned up and I got to pay Jay's Automotive who finally pronounced it unsalvageable.

Uncle Paul was a dapper little guy on Carolyn's side of the family who became disinterested in further marriage when his wife chose the company of other men. He lived alone and slowly went legally blind until laser surgery was able to rectify his eyesight, but not before he had quit driving. We bought his car, a 1975 MonteCarlo - the last year of the round headlights. The car was a sled by every comparison, a classic example of Detroit's heavy metal past. It was, however, in pristine condition and Uncle Paul didn't want too much for it. Since we had given the Coronet to Jazzy, I had been once again looking for something safe for my son to start out with. I had the Monte Carlo painted a 1979 Ford metal-flake blue and replaced the vinyl roof in a lighter shade. The black interior was like new; the back seat had seldom even been used. Not long after, my son decided that he couldn't afford to feed this behemoth. Driving his pals all over Rhode Island on a weekend, he couldn't keep the car going at 12 miles to a gallon. I thought this would keep my son close; it only kept him complaining. It seems that he was buying all the gas since it was bad form to ask any of his rich friends to contribute. When my friend Joe Cap put his wife's Toyota up for sale, I snapped it up. I put the MonteCarlo in the paper to show on a Saturday and when I went out that morning to clean it up, there was a guardrail stripe all the way down the passenger side. I ran upstairs to roust my comatose child:

"WHAT THE HELL HAPPENED TO THE CAR?!!"

"Aren't you even glad that I'm O.K.?"

Whatever the story, it wasn't going to be the truth and I had to call everyone who was coming to look at this jewel to explain what had happened. I sold the car to another friend on the job who laughed and said that his daughter would just match the other side. I got next to nothing for the car and KJ got his Toyota.

Bob finally got his head out of the sand just when we thought he never would and fell headlong into the world of theatre. Once an actor but never again, Bob roamed far and wide on tour as a techie where he took an electrical jolt that Carolyn felt all the way across the country when it happened. In Vegas, Bob kept company with a stunning singer and a girl with perfectly natural purple hair and he essentially learned to appreciate having a real future in projection and sound. By the time Colleen arrived, Bob had almost grown himself up and only needed a little finishing. She could work with that.

The Bentley College Experience deteriorated almost from the beginning when intramural track meets and keg parties took precedence. A broken down Jeep found its' way into our conflict by way of simply appearing and it sucked up every spare dime of my son's allocation. When the accounting degree and the MBA morphed into marketing and the grades belied any real commitment, the Bentley College Experience was replaced with the option of any second choice. That opportunity was decidedly refused and my son moved on to make his own way. The college loan went with exWife, who once again had married well.

What I never expected was to stand accused of having only my own interest at heart, that I would seize control and try to dictate any future I imagined for my son. That was Dad's intent - never mine. The fact that I would not allow the child to determine our foreseeable future stands against me. Never had I felt so defeated in everything I ever tried to accomplish on his behalf. I never abandoned my son as he would suggest. It was only after he took everything there was that I stopped going the extra mile. There was more that we were willing to do, but not without some acknowledgement of the missteps we had all made thus far.

We were always headed west, me and Carolyn; it was just a question of when. The back problem had finally outpaced the means of modern medicine to provide any relief. There was no surgical intervention to be had at that time; indeed there wasn't even CAT-Scan or MRI when I first got injured. There were only pills and nerve blocks and more pills to counteract the gastrointestinal damage from the original pills. I wish I was done with pills. Dr. Reardon said that the only real relief would be to get off of the rescue truck – to stop compounding the problem with repeated injury and strain. I could try to outlast it or I could start the endless process that would lead to a permanent disability pension from the fire department. Physical therapy and acupuncture and apitherapy would help to bridge the time I needed to retire from rescue with a regular pension; I was adamant about finishing my time and *not* going off disabled. Our new life in the west might require additional employment and no one hires a disabled lower back. I was out quite a bit towards the end, and time at the station would never be without the back support and the TEN's unit that sent regular electrical charges as I tried to fry the angry nerve. I managed to complete my 20 years without the disability label, but if someone way back when had told me I'd be gone in 20, I never would have believed it. I was 42.

Carolyn is entitled to a degree of consideration concerning all of us Larrivees. It was Carolyn who was bed-side when Gramp woke up from by-pass surgery. It was Carolyn who had attended to Dad's illness and to Mom's death. It was Carolyn who heard first hand from Dad about how he needed to get right with the family and it was Carolyn who was most disappointed by Dad's failure to do so. Everybody else knew that he never would. It was Carolyn who often got between me and my son, and usually on his behalf if she thought that in any way I should have been more understanding. And it was Carolyn who got from him the worst of what was intended to hurt us both.

It took most of her life for Carolyn to learn that the rest of the world doesn't share her integrity. Carolyn doesn't misrepresent the truth because she doesn't fear the truth - never has. She might allow an omission to spare my feelings or herself an argument but over all, she's pretty straight up. My son maintains that Carolyn serves as something of a double agent between us, speaking only the truth that suits the situation. Legions of co-workers and subordinates and others who know us well would say otherwise. Carolyn has courageously and repeatedly put our livelihood and her professional reputation on the line in the interest of justice and integrity. There is only the difference between right and wrong, and Carolyn has never wavered - not once – even when it hurt us.

SonsWife writes to me about her education to obstinate Larrivee's - about how what comes to mind is said, her words exactly. Our first thought isn't always our best but it manages to escape us anyway. We never mean to offend, except for when we do and it comes down like a hammer. Me and David are afflicted with that certain lack of diplomacy and one of the twins never could be around polite society. All of Dad's kids except for Steven could be defined with the words "obtuse" and "inappropriate" in a sentence that would also describe a distinct lack of consideration. Those who love us quickly learn that the rancor is usually overstated and it also quickly dissolves, but that doesn't mean that it hurts any less to hear. In our world, some people are just too easily offended. Others would say that we can be abusive.

The written word takes quite a different form. You get to say exactly what you mean over a little more time and to change it or soften it or abandon the thought altogether when it really doesn't matter or if it's just plain wrong. It is a therapeutic process that requires a continuing re-assessment of the values and the bias that I have trouble moving off of, even when I was wrong in the altogether. Too bad Dad never wrote – it might have explained a lot. Me and David eventually get it; Dad never, ever looked back or offered apology or repentance for any of his offensively poor judgment. Nor has my son. I have correspondence that I would like to believe he has since reconsidered but the evidence would indicate otherwise. The theme and the projection is repeatedly asserted without change or redress and he clearly still believes in all of the convictions he has thus far drawn and imparted to others as well. I have finally come to grips as I've needed to with the life I was assigned to fulfill. This wasn't always the case and I do indeed recall how angry and bitter I had become over circumstances beyond my control. Now I discover that this intemperance is thematic throughout generations of our kind, that the apes became people faster than our Larrivee's could ever learn to get along. The apple never falls too far from the tree.

Gramp would always say that it was my duty as a son to honor my father and he was old and wise and good and true. But Gramp could never come to grips with the measure of degradation that I described of Dad's household. The letters next to sonsWife and her chosen profession would suggest that she is a considered expert in parent/child relationships. It is her contention that the parent should undertake the greater role in fixing what's broken - no matter the cause - whatever it takes. I suspect that she has never caused her parents even a moment's grief.

My son harbors no reservations about giving offense or expressing his contempt while he dismisses his own role as merely reflexive. I have come to understand that what he wants for me is the same disconnect that had meant so little to Dad. It took years for me to come to grips with that as our forever and then the scab was ripped away when I first heard from his wife. My son advises that I must take my medicine or find peace in my cowardice; all this and more from someone who could only take from the relationship, as though I should have only contrition to offer. At one time I did, and I had hoped it would be the last of our disparaging words. All these years later, I don't know who my son became and I can only speak about who we once were or perhaps, of what we never shared. He was my son until he stopped calling me his dad, quite a long time ago. I have been weighed, measured, and found to be wanting. That too was a long time ago. It has been long enough once again to say that everybody seems to have moved on.

So now we are done with it, me *and* Carolyn. It's time for us to re-connect with why we came to the west. It has been many years of us having to endure my father and my son and all of the associated Larrivee syndrome. I regret that his children are just somebody else's kids and my son, a product of his mother or perhaps just of his very own self. SonsWife can never accept that I feel this way but my life has been a collection of disaffection from my father and from my son, even though I stood for all the right stuff. I'm just not having any more. Likewise, I no longer try to imagine his life or any place for me in it. Had I never married Carolyn - or anybody else for that matter - my son still wouldn't care any more or any less about my feelings than he does at this time. I wouldn't let his mommy come home.

Mobile Intensive Cab Company
Captain Gerry Larrivee (Retired)

A Heart in Need

We were all out on the apparatus floor when the call came in for a "woman passed out". The rescue had been dispatched without benefit of an engine company and as we ran to the truck, Fireman Bill who was the engine Lieutenant summoned his crew to do likewise. Without hesitation, Engine 4 was out the door with us – even before I could get on the air to ask for them.

We headed for an office building that is just down the road from the fire station and we got there just inside of a minute. The building was marked only by a street number at the front and there were identical entrances on each side. "Suite 2A" might be on the second floor or it might be on either side of the building; there was no way to know. We entered on the right and Fireman Bill and his crew entered on the left. As luck would have it there was no interior connection and we had to re-trace our steps all the way around to the other side where the engine crew was already getting report.

A trim young lady in Spandex was nearly passed out on the floor and she was drenched in cold sweat. She was somewhat coherent and breathless and she told me in a whisper that she felt extremely weak, like she was going to die. We assured her otherwise and Fireman Bill related everything he had been told so far. Feeling for her pulse, there was none at the wrist and only a faint palpation at the carotid. Her heart was racing along fast and thready which explained the absence of an audible blood pressure.

The back story is that the girl had been out running and suddenly didn't feel so well. She had immediate need of bathroom facilities so she ducked into this office complex because her sister worked there. Emerging from the ladies room, she suddenly crumped and now here we were, trying to figure out how bad this all really was. She had no medical history to speak of and only takes birth control pills. Her breathing was labored but her lungs were clear and she only seemed like someone who could use a little hydration or a little sugar or both. Since we could do it quickly, we moved her right to the truck and put her into Trendelenberg, the shock position. Almost immediately she complained of pressure in her chest and her breathing became even more distressed. We abandoned Trendelenberg and began a full advanced life support work-up for now it appeared that despite the incredible odds against it, we were faced with a serious cardiac disorder.

We set her up on a non-rebreather mask at 100% oxygen while other hands tore open an I.V. assembly and began to bleed it down. The ECG monitor was skipping along, almost too fast to count and it seemed that we needed to be in more of a hurry. Fireman Bill stood outside the truck at the side door where he cut tape and opened prep pads. We exchange glances often when the pressure is on and Bill and his crew have always had a pretty good read on what needs to happen next. We elected to take a man from Engine 4, just in case we suddenly needed to initiate CPR.

Our young patient was awake and having a little more chest discomfort and she still didn't have a palpable blood pressure. We established communications with the ER en route and we asked for a special room where this emergency could be quickly evaluated. She was breathing a little better on the oxygen but we set up for intubation anyway. The hospital issued no orders and we were only a few minutes away and aside from a little anxiety, transport was routine.

Once we arrived at the hospital, a code room was waiting and a medical team assembled. We decide to stick around to see what the diagnosis would turn out to be or to appreciate what we might have missed. The ER team was able to get a blood pressure of 90/70 and the patient wasn't quite so diaphoretic. While they were calling for all of the routine blood work, chest X-rays, etc., someone called out that her pressure had fallen to 70/30. In order to validate that reading, they took her pressure with a cuff. They could no longer hear it and now she had become unconscious and her ECG was erratic. There was no palpable pulse. They called a "code", the patient was intubated, pronounced to be stable enough, and rushed off to the coronary care unit. The next step would be a cardiac catheterization to try to determine what in fact had occurred.

Our young lady was found to have a virus that had invaded her heart. The heart had become terminally weakened which grossly compromised her systemic circulation, eventually leading to multi-organ failure. There wasn't any cure to be found and heart transplants were not then done in Rhode Island. Now the challenge was to keep her alive, find a donor heart, and get her to Boston. Extraordinary measures were employed to ensure that she would survive the trip. An intra-aortic balloon (a device that assists the heart from within) was inserted and she was otherwise prepared to go. The helicopter was waiting and the emergency flight crew had arrived on the floor when she arrested for what would be the last time. There would be no replacement heart, no second chance – nothing more to be done.

Aerobically fit 26 year old females are not generally featured within the cardiac risk profile. Being young and athletic was probably what kept her going for as long as she had. Others would usually just slide right into cardiac arrest and never recover or if they did, it would not be without physiological or neurological impairment. This young lady and those who loved her lost everything that day in very short order. Here today; gone tomorrow. Believe it.

LaVergne, TN USA
08 December 2010

207800LV00003B/9/P